INVASION!

Ian White

INVASION! (First Edition)

ISBN 978-0-646-87311-4
First Edition published 2023

Cover

Quite some time was spent considering appropriate images for the cover of this book. Should it be an illustration of Governor Arthur Phillip raising the British flag at Sydney Cove on 26th January 1788? Would it perhaps be appropriate to use one showing red-coated British soldiers advancing through the Australian bush with muskets and bayonets at the ready or early settlers massacring Aboriginal people in the corn fields? An image of Lachlan Macquarie's statue in Sydney's Hyde Park covered in red paint, representing Aboriginal blood thrown by Aboriginal activists, could have been used. There were many other options, some too graphic to have been seriously considered. Yet, finally it was decided that a stark black and white cover would say it better than any image because, at its heart, it is a black-and-white issue – an ongoing black-and-white conflict.

Ian White

REVIEW

Hats off to Ian White for having the courage to write and publish his latest book, *Invasion!* Whatever views we may hold about the Indigenous people of our nation, their past treatment and present and future well-being, I believe this is a truly valuable resource that informs, elucidates and, yes, challenges. In *Invasion!* Ian White seeks to paint an accurate picture of the often difficult and violent relationship between the Aboriginals and the early British settlers in our land and also of the legacy this clash of European and Indigenous culture has left behind that still impacts our nation today.

Ian White's thoughtful, meticulous research is obvious in his frequent references to primary sources from the early days of British settlement in New South Wales and also to the works of other authors knowledgeable on the subject. However, it is his empathy with and compassion for the Indigenous people of our nation, along with his sincere desire to advocate for the righting of past wrongs against them, that may succeed in leaving the most lasting impression on any who read this volume. May *Invasion!* be received with due respect and given the thoughtful consideration it well deserves.

Jo-Anne Berthelsen, writer and speaker
www.jo-anneberthelsen.com

Other Books by this Author

Brand New Every Morning
A daily guide to reading the Bible in one year.

The Mustard Seed
God's plan for New Creation

Glass Half Full
An uplifting book of encouragement for Christians and for non-Christians alike as we attempt to deal with the rollercoaster ride of life.

Matthew James Everingham – Convict of the First Fleet
The life and times of Matthew James Everingham, convicted in the Old Bailey at fifteen years of age and transported to New South Wales on the First Fleet. The first book in the trilogy about the Everingham Dynasty

Elizabeth Rymes – A Remarkable Life
The life and times of Elizabeth Rymes, a truly remarkable woman pioneer in the early colonial days of Australia. The second book in the trilogy about the Everingham Dynasty.

The Woodbury Line – An Australian Convict Family
The third book in the trilogy about the Everingham Dynasty. The saga of one branch of the Woodbury family, descended from the eldest daughter of Matthew and Elizabeth Everingham, Sarah (aka Sally), who married ex-convict Richard Woodbury and commenced the Woodbury line of descendants.

Details of all books can be found at
www.themustardseed.net.au/books

DEDICATION

To the memory of those Indigenous Australians who
suffered and to those who still suffer.

Ian White

The author affirms the dispossession of the original
Indigenous inhabitants of this land and acknowledges
their unique status as Australia's First Peoples, their
cultures, histories, ongoing relationships and obligations
to the land.

The very ink with which all history is written is
merely fluid prejudice.

– Mark Twain

CONTENTS

ACKNOWLEDGEMENTS

Whenever I complete a new book, I feel humbled – humbled because I recognise that there were many along the way who helped get the book to the point where it was ready to be sent to the printers. With the completion of this book, however, I find myself consumed by yet another feeling – one that I have not felt before and one that I find difficult to define. It is somewhere between humility and shame, perhaps a combination of the two, because this book does shame me. It should shame all white Australians, and if it does not, then I have failed in my endeavour. And so, the first acknowledgement that should be made here is to the Indigenous peoples of this land

As I researched and worked my way through the writing of this book, I spoke with many Indigenous Australians, young and old, and gathered from them their sense of loss, almost invariably expressed with a sense of deep abiding grief. The older generation often spoke of the dispossession of their ancestors and of the many different injustices inflicted upon them by white settlement, including the massacres of their ancestors. They spoke also of their ongoing sense of deprivation and bereavement from the land and of the racism they still endure.

The range of attitudes and responses from the younger generation covered a significantly wider spectrum. Many of them spoke of a deep sense of loss, yet often they found it difficult to define. It appeared to me to be a loss of *belonging* together with a sense of ongoing disentitlement. Others were more militant and spoke with some anger about the massacres of their ancestors, about their loss of sovereignty over their land and about the myriad of injustices perpetrated upon them.

As a non-Indigenous writer and as a descendant of white convict settlers, I expected to encounter some degree of hostility, of censure and condemnation – perhaps accusations that in some way I was an agent of their dispossession and of their ongoing plight. Yet, not once did I feel that I was being personally criticised for the acts of my forebears – not even by the militant youth amongst them. Yes, they spoke with despondency, anguish, and sometimes with ill-concealed anger, but never with reproachfulness. I was left with the distinct conviction that they were people of a gentle race and that they were pleased to be sharing their anthropological history and culture with a non-Indigenous person seeking to understand the circumstances that they face daily. I thank them all as the respected First Nations peoples of Australia for the help they gave me in coming to an understanding of their plight and of their resilience and forbearance.

George Vanags is a longstanding friend and a colleague from my teaching days. George and I taught languages together at a secondary school in the suburbs of Melbourne where George was also Head of the Humanities Department, teaching Australian history. When I turned my attention to the writing of a book relating to the early colonial history of this land, George was the first person I reached out to for help and I appreciated his willingness to read the first draft and offer many suggestions which made this a better book than it was when first passed to him. Thank you, George.

Barry and Elizabeth Gardner have been wonderful friends for more than fifty years and I owe them an enormous debt of gratitude for so many things during that time – they have been like family to me. Barry and Elizabeth not only read the manuscript and made suggestions which helped get this book to its final form but were also invaluable intermediary contacts with others. Thank you Barry and Elizabeth.

Jo-Anne Berthelsen is my 'go-to' editor, tasked with turning my sometimes rough manuscripts into readable books. Oh, Jo-Anne, where would I be without you? I am so grateful that we met and that we have had opportunities to work together on my books. I thank you once again for your professionalism and your painstaking work.

Ian White

INTRODUCTION

I like to think that there must have been somebody amongst the early colonisers of this country who empathised with the Indigenous peoples of Australia, who respected them as the First Nations Peoples of this land and who recognised and honoured their cultures, their histories, their rightful place as owners and custodians of the land and their ongoing relationships and obligations to the land. But this book is not about him.

I need to make it clear at the outset that I am not an Indigenous Australian. I am descended from white convict ancestors – those whom Indigenous Australians would probably and quite correctly refer to as invaders. Yet, I love this broad land, I am proud of the land of my birth and proud to call myself an Australian. There are some things, however, of which I am truly ashamed, and those matters will become evident to readers as they progress through this book.

I hope Indigenous readers will find me to be a person who acknowledges and affirms the dispossession of the original Indigenous inhabitants of this land and one who recognises and empathises with the ongoing sense of deprivation and bereavement amongst present day Indigenous Australians. I find it impossible to reconcile the manner in which our white Australian forebears treated the Indigenous peoples of this land and am saddened by the fact that, almost two and a half centuries later, we have not been able to heal the black-white divide in our society.

Even today in the twenty-first century, there remains the perception within the white Australian community that the Aboriginal people in the late eighteenth and early nineteenth centuries did not actively resist the establishment and expansion of the British colony in New South Wales. Perhaps this misguided perception is derived from the journals of Captain James Cook and botanist Joseph Banks wherein they erroneously wrote that the natives of New Holland were a timid and passive people who could not be expected to respond with armed resistance when challenged. Perhaps it arises from the fact that, whilst this country has many monuments to memorialise the early Governors of New South Wales, British sovereigns and other prominent Europeans, even British playwrights and poets, there are no monuments commemorating the Aboriginal leaders of what historians now call "The Frontier Wars" – a disparity which urgently needs to be addressed. Perhaps, in part, it also arises from the fact that the sustained and systematic expansion of white settlement into Aboriginal Country, and the resulting conflict, is not adequately addressed in our school curriculums.

Regardless of how that perception gained common acceptance, it is wrong. The Indigenous people of this land staunchly and fiercely resisted the expansion of white settlement into their Country and their story needs to be told and accepted by white Australia if we are ever to move forward in true reconciliation.

Some present day Indigenous Australians, I know, feel very strongly that non-Indigenous people should not be writing the Aboriginal story. That, they say, is their story to tell. I try to understand those sentiments, yet I disagree even whilst knowing that Indigenous people will say to me, "You've not walked in our shoes. You've not lived the life that white Australia has inflicted upon us. How *can* you understand?" In many ways, they are right. But, one thing I know – that to silence white Australians from speaking out on issues relating to Indigenous dispossession and the injustices inflicted upon them by our white forebears is to perpetuate the racial divide between us. As a non-Indigenous writer and one who is removed from the colonial era by more than two hundred years, I have indeed found it challenging to write about the Indigenous peoples of that era and I do sometimes pause to wonder whether I have any authority to do so. Indeed, I have been explicitly told I do not have any authority to tell that story. Yet the story burns within me and I feel compelled to act on my convictions. I have attempted to write about the Indigenous peoples of this land with the honour and the respect they are owed and if there be anything in the following pages which offends Indigenous Australians then that has certainly not been my intent and I unreservedly apologise for any such offence unwittingly given, including by omission.

I am the first to admit that my knowledge of Aboriginal psyche, culture and the pain of dispossession, discrimination, racism and alienation is very limited. I have not lived that – I can barely imagine it – and I know I cannot tell the complete story as it should and must be told. I embark on this project knowing I cannot adequately describe the pain of ongoing estrangement and disassociation from the mainstream white Australian community. And I know that, when writing about the massacres of the ancestors of Indigenous Australians, about the decimation of their people through infectious diseases brought to these shores by colonists, about the abduction of their women and children and about the genocidal intent of many settlers, as a non-Indigenous writer, I am going to get things wrong. There is little doubt about that. I am prepared to risk those errors, however, because I know that the people of this nation, black and white, are desperately in need of a full and genuine reconciliation and I believe such reconciliation can only be achieved when the interactions of white Australian colonists and First Nations Peoples are explored and told by people of good will, black *and* white. To be part of that process is the task I have set myself with the writing of this book. Criticise me for that if you will.

This book, I suspect, is not going to make me popular – not popular amongst white Australians because they are likely to feel I have gone too far and have raised issues of guilt and uncomfortable questions for them and not popular amongst Indigenous Australians because they are likely to feel I have not gone far enough. I did not reach this position by setting out to record a balanced viewpoint – I do not think it possible to do this when dealing with any issue which, in itself, shows such an obvious state of imbalance.

Instead, I set out to address the colonial policies, attitudes and actions – whether based on fear, misunderstandings, ignorance or an unwavering sense of ethnic superiority – which gave rise to the painful divide that exists between black and white Australians today. If in the process my writing falls somewhere other than the balanced viewpoint, then so be it. There are lessons to be learned from that.

I was advised to use a softer or more palatable title for this book. *Invasion!*, people told me, is such an emotive word which can be seen as judgmental and accusatory, especially when readers themselves are identified as the invaders. I recognise and understand that and I did consider other titles, knowing that in bookstores many white Australians would turn their back on this book and refuse to pick it up, simply because of the title.

This advice caused something of a dilemma for me, which I pondered over for quite some time. I did want white Australians to read the book – it was largely for them that it was written. Yet, at the same time, I felt that a softer title, perhaps something like *White Settlement of Australia* or *The Colonisation of Australia*, would be pandering to the already heavily skewed attitudes on this issue within the Australian community – skewed in favour of white Australians, partly due to weight of numbers and partly because of the inherent and

4

long-held attitudes of white Australians on this issue. I was aware, also, that to have softened the title would have necessitated taking a more gentle approach to the writing of the story by softening other emotive words in this book – words like "massacres", "decapitations", "mass murders" and "genocide".

Yes, let me acknowledge here that I also wanted to use the shock value of the title. "Invasion" is a word frequently used by Aboriginal activists and commentators. Yet, not many non-Indigenous commentators or writers use the word in this context. I wanted to put it out there, to unambiguously put the issue front and centre before the eyes of white Australians and if they are shocked and angered by that, then the consequences be damned.

"Racism" is another emotive word although, alongside words like "massacres", "mass murders", "decapitations" and "genocide", it seems almost genteel. I think about that as I ask, "Is Australia, today, a racist country?" I have absolutely no doubt that the vast majority of white Australians would answer "No", some quite emphatically. I know that for a fact because, since I first entertained the idea of writing this book, it is a question I have asked of many people, black and white.

Some white respondents have stated, and I am sure all readers will have heard this said, "I'm not a racist, but … ". Let me say here, the word "but" has no place in any discussion about racism. One is a racist or one is not. There are no "buts". Yet, ask that question of any Australian Aboriginal or any Australian of foreign ethnicity and, if they have the courage to express their true feelings, their answers may be very different and more than a little confronting. Again, I know, for I have spent the last two years asking that very question to such Australians.

When speaking of Aboriginal people, one of the most frequently heard racist comments coming from white Australians is that Aboriginal people are lazy, that they don't want to work and that they sponge on the national welfare system with a sense of entitlement. I felt my anger rising within me even as I typed that sentence. Some – a minority – may be as described in that sentence, yet the same could be said of white Australians in greater numbers and with greater veracity. There are such people in every community, black and white, but to label an entire race of people as such is clearly a racist attitude. It is the erroneous expression of a racist stereotypical view which remains common within the white Australian community – it is hurtful and demeaning to current day Indigenous Australians and it is not new. *The Sydney Gazette & New South Wales Advertiser* was influencing the opinions of its readers, in the first decade of the nineteenth century with frequent reports that labelled the natives in that way.

> *They despoil the settler of his crop and reap by stealth and open violence the produce of* **a tract they are themselves too indolent to cultivate.**[1] (emphasis added)

Thus, such pervasive racist comments were absorbed into the white Australian consciousness from earliest colonial days and endure today. This division in our nation along black and white lines did not happened overnight. It has not been the product of the twenty-first century, the twentieth century nor even most of the nineteenth century. Its origins lie deeply rooted in the last two decades of the eighteenth century and the first two decades of the nineteenth century – a time when Britain was establishing a penal colony in a land as far away from Britain as possible. To do so, of course, meant finding a land that could be declared vacant and there for the taking, thus giving rise to the term *terra-nullius*.

Terra-nullius? Nobody's land? They wished it was, they said it was, and it would have been convenient for them had it so been, but it wasn't. Yet, the British government and the British Colonial Office deemed it to be so, based in part on their innate sense of superiority over the native peoples of lands they claimed as their own. In the case of Australia, they specifically justified their actions by declaring that the Great Southern Land, New Holland, was not legally recognised as a sovereign nation. Hence, it belonged to nobody.

The British, of course, were not the only ones procuring foreign lands at the expense of Indigenous peoples. The French, the Dutch and the Spanish were competing in the land grab with equal disregard for the dispossession of the Indigenous peoples. In most instances, including in the case of Australia, they knew the land was occupied. They knew it was somebody's land, yet the colonial offices in the respective home governments rationalised their acts of invasion partly on the grounds that they were bringing a higher, more refined form of civilisation to backward and primitive peoples who should be eternally grateful for the magnanimous gift being bestowed upon them, whether they wanted it or not. Besides, the invaders invariably had a more developed home industrial base, an industrial base through which they had been able to develop more effective weapons than the Indigenous peoples. Surely, they believed, their superior commercial and industrial base, together with their superior weapons, meant that it was quite reasonable for them to assert their superiority.

In current day Australia, rationalising the invasion of this country continues by many, perhaps most, in the white Australian community. One of the rationalisations most commonly heard claims, quite legitimately, that issues of national integrity were quite different two centuries ago. "Well, it was a long time ago," apologists say. "We should not judge the actions of the past by our twenty-first century values." To which I ask, "Why not?" Wrong acts are not contingent on timing. Yes, such a policy of national expansion through the dispossession of others may have been universally accepted in the late eighteenth century, but that is not to say it was right. Slavery was also commonly accepted in those times – do we say slavery was right? We might now look on colonisation and dispossession with hindsight and through our twenty-first century sensibilities, yet when we say, "It is wrong now," we must also say, "It was wrong then."

Other rationalisations are frequently raised to mitigate the acts of the early colonists. Recently, I found myself in a discussion about colonisation and dispossession with a very good friend, a white Australian and a fine man whom I respect greatly. Yet, we disagreed strongly on this issue. My friend said to me, "If we (meaning the British) had not colonised this land, some other nation would have done so, probably the French." Well, yes probably, but should we evaluate our own integrity and justify our own actions by making comparisons with what some other nation may or may not have done? We are our own people, and the actions of others should be irrelevant when assessing the morality of our national acts. Were others to launch an antisemitic pogrom, does that mean we would be justified in doing the same and that we should show the way by being leaders in doing so? Really? Is that the way for any nation to measure its integrity and morality?

Another rationalisation of the issue goes along the lines of "I'm a modern day Australian, born and bred in this land. I had no choice in that and I cannot be held responsible for the actions of my ancestors who came to this country at least six generations ago." That is absolutely true, and this book does not set out to hold current day white Australians responsible for the acts of their forebears. It *does* set out to make white Australians aware of those acts, to call on them to acknowledge the wrongs that were done to the Indigenous peoples by our white ancestors, to apologise and to move forward together with current day Indigenous Australians in a spirit of reconciliation.

There is yet another white response to this land's history of invasion and dispossession – not so much a rationalisation but, rather, almost a plea to put it behind us, unresolved, and just move on. "Let's just forget about the past," some say. "It was a long time ago and we cannot change the past, so let's just look to the future and move on together." It proposes a simplistic and convenient whitewashing, literally, of past offences and says to Indigenous people, "For God's sake, just get over it and move on!" I recall a recent conversation with a wonderful friend, a man whom I hold in high regard, who told me that Aboriginal people need to "learn to forgive". The problem with that perspective is that forgiveness that leads to true and lasting reconciliation is a two-way transaction. It requires offenders, or their descendants, to acknowledge that wrongs have been done and that forgiveness is needed. Indeed, complete forgiveness, in any situation, requires an act of repentance on the part of those seeking forgiveness and that, almost certainly, involves an apology. In short, such forgiveness must be asked for.

The Indigenous peoples of this continent have never received a national apology for the invasion of their land, for their dispossession, for the massacres of their ancestors and for the myriad other offences perpetrated against them as part of the white colonisation of this land. They have never seen any act of national repentance or contrition in respect to these issues and so, for them, calls to "just move on" amount to little more than a slap in the face – a national insult. The Indigenous peoples of this land have never ceded sovereignty of their land and have never signed any treaty. Indeed, they have not been offered any treaty, and they continue, in the twenty-first century, to protest against the invasion of their lands and what, in international law, would be considered crimes against humanity.

So here we are, black and white Australians trying to reconcile past offences and trying to find ways to live together – some, on both sides, trying harder than others. It will take a coming together of the minds, it will take an act of national contrition and it will take education entailing a fresh look at the actions of the British colonists on these shores. And that, largely, is the intent of this book.

Whilst recognising that massacres of Aboriginal people continued well into the twentieth century, and that racism and discriminatory social policies continue today, this book will focus on the crucible of ongoing estrangement between black and white Australians – the tumultuous years of the five authoritarian governors of New South Wales: Captain Arthur Phillip, Captain John Hunter, Captain Philip Gidley King, Captain William Bligh and Major General Lachlan Macquarie. Some of it will be confronting, especially for white Australians, but that is the purpose of this book which, I hope, might play some small part in the much needed truth-telling and healing process.

1

RECONNAISSANCE

29th April 1770

Generations of Australian school children, this author being one of them, were taught that Captain James Cook discovered Australia in 1770. The Aboriginal people would challenge that statement; indeed, they would be insulted by it and some would be incensed by it. They have a point – after all, they have been here for more than sixty thousand years. I wonder, today, how those Aboriginal children in my junior school classes in country New South Wales felt about being taught of Cook's discovery of their land. How did that sit with what their parents taught them at home – that they were part of the oldest continuous culture on the face of the planet?

Cook's statue in Sydney's Hyde Park carries the inscription on the rear side of the monument pedestal: "DISCOVERED THIS TERRITORY 1770". That inscription is fading in comparison with the inscriptions on the other three sides of the pedestal and can be easily missed, and it may be an intentional move by the park and city authorities to let those words fade from history – an easier and less controversial course of action than openly declaring the statement to be wrong and removing it. If no restorative work on that inscription is done soon, it may well fade away completely – so much the better. Perhaps, after this happens, a more appropriate inscription may be something like "Visited these shores in 1770 and charted the east coast of the Australian continent". That, at least, would be true.

Yet, even if one discounts the Aboriginal presence, as many were and are apt to do, then even that fading statement can be applied only to the east coast of Australia, for Cook was far from the first European to land on the Australian continent.

In March 1606, Willem Janszoon and his crew aboard the VOC[2] ship *Duyfken* charted around two hundred miles of the west coast of Cape York peninsular and made the first recorded landing of Europeans on what is now known as the Australian continent. Ten years later, in 1616, Dirk Hartog aboard the *Eendracht* sighted and landed upon an island off the west coast of the continent which he named Dirk Hartog Island. There, Hartog left a pewter plate, "The Hartog Plate", recording details of his visit. Then, in 1619, Frederik de Houtman and Jacob Dedel aboard the *Dordrect* and the *Amsterdam* visited the west coast near what is now the present-day mouth of the Swan River, and Rottnest Island.

In 1642, VOC Commander Abel Janszoon Tasman sailed the *Heemskerck* along the south coast of the continent, proving it was not connected to any land further south. When he encountered what is now Tasmania, rough seas forbade a landing so Tasman had a member of his crew swim ashore and plant a pole marked "VOC" with the Dutch flag. Tasman named the place Van Diemen's Land. Numerous other landings, mostly by Dutch sailors of the VOC, are recorded along the western and northern coasts of the continent, pre-dating the arrival of Cook on the east coast in 1770.

Cook, in fact, was not even the first Englishman to set foot on the Australian continent. That claim to fame went to William Dampier, English explorer, pirate, privateer, navigator and naturalist who became the first Englishman to explore parts of what is today Australia. On 6th August 1699, Dampier had visited and named Shark Bay on the western coast of the continent. There, Dampier landed and began producing the first known detailed record of Australian flora and fauna, pre-dating the work of botanist Joseph Banks who would accompany Cook on the *Endeavour*. Dampier also landed on

12

Dirk Hartog Island and at Lagrange Bay, south of present-day Broome, where he was attacked by Indigenous people. He then sailed north before turning east to chart the Dampier Strait. Because of the deteriorating state of his ship, the *Roebuck*, Dampier was forced to abandon his plans to chart the east coast of New Holland when he was less than a hundred miles from it. That task would be left to Lieutenant James Cook on *HMB Endeavour*.

What Cook can rightly lay claim to is that he was the first European to sight and land on the east coast of the Australian continent.

Captain James Cook, or Lieutenant James Cook as he then was, embarked on his first voyage of discovery on behalf of both the British Admiralty and the Royal Society of London for Improving Natural Knowledge. He and his crew departed England on 27th May 1768 with instructions to sail into the South Pacific and there to record the transit of Venus across the sun. In addition to his Naval pay, Cook would receive a gratuity of one hundred guineas from the Royal Society.

Cook and his crew on *HMB Endeavour* rounded Cape Horn and proceeded into the South Pacific. They arrived at a point near Tahiti on 13th April 1769 where, in accordance with his instructions, Cook would record his observations of the 1769 transit. It was intended, or hoped, that such observations would aid in measuring the distance of the earth from the sun. As it turned out, Cook's observations, combined with observations by others in different places, were not as elucidating as had been hoped.

However, with that part of his instructions completed, Cook then opened further sealed orders from the Admiralty for the second purpose of his voyage – to search the South Pacific for the assumed existence of the huge southern continent of *Terra Australis*. It is at this point that Cook's instructions, actually termed "hints" from the Royal Society, become relevant to us. The president of the Royal Society, James Douglas, had given Cook hints that related to how the people of new lands should be treated. In these hints, Cook was instructed to *"respect Indigenous land occupation"* and to *"exercise utmost patience and forbearance when dealing with such people"*. He was also exhorted to impress upon his crew that they were *"to do no harm to any Indigenous inhabitants they might meet"*.[3]

After circumnavigating and charting the islands of New Zealand, Cook and the *Endeavour* continued westwards where, on 19th April 1770, he made the first recorded European sighting of the eastern coastline of New Holland at a point which he named Point Hicks. From Point Hicks, *Endeavour* continued northwards just a few miles offshore, with Cook charting and naming costal formations as he went. On 29th April 1770, *Endeavour* dropped anchor in a broad bay which, a few days later, Cook would name Botany Bay.

That same morning, Sunday 29th April 1770, as a landing party approached the shoreline, they were confronted by two Gweagal warriors of the Eora nation making threatening gestures with raised spears and shouting *"warra warra wai"*. Cook, quite reasonably, interpreted the words in conjunction with the threatening spears to mean "go away", but this was incorrect. They were, in fact, a phrase from Gweagal dreaming relating to stories of the return of *guwinj* (spirit or ghost) from the afterlife, which, according to the dreaming tales, would arrive in low-lying clouds. The Gweagal people saw the *Endeavour* as a ship carried by low-lying clouds because of its billowing, white sails.[4]

During the confrontation between the Gweagal warriors and the landing party, one of the accompanying sailors fired with musket upon the Gweagal warriors. One of the natives was struck by a musket ball although, from the words of Cook's journal, the impression given is that the warrior was not seriously wounded.[5]

The Eora people showed no interest in clothing, beads and other trinkets which Cook's landing party left on the beach for them but launched several spears, 'darts' as Cook called them, to rebuff and repulse the newcomers. It is likely that Cook's landing party may have misinterpreted the apparent threatening actions of the two native warriors and, had they proceeded a little more judiciously, an opening for more constructive interactions may have eventuated. Shooting at one of the natives had been a precipitous step.

Notwithstanding the fact that the natives had been fired upon, wounding one of them – not an auspicious beginning – Cook seems to have been intent on complying with his hints from the Royal Society to *"exercise utmost patience and forbearance when dealing with the natives"*. It does appear that he treated the people he encountered with a level of respect not found in other European explorers of the time and, whilst his efforts were rebuffed, he did seek to establish friendly relations and interaction with the Indigenous people. On 30th April 1770, seemingly in despair, he recorded in his journal:

All they seemed to want was for us to be gone.[6]

On the morning of 6th May 1770, as Cook was preparing his ship for departure from Botany Bay, he wrote in his journal about the Aboriginals:

We could know but very little of their custom as we were never able to form any connections with them.[7]

That same day, Cook acceded to the perceived desires of the natives and sailed *Endeavour* out of Botany Bay. He recorded his departure from Botany Bay by writing in his journal:

Having seen everything this place afforded we at daylight in the morning weighed with a light breeze at NW and put to sea.[8]

It is commonly believed by many Australians that, at Botany Bay, James Cook claimed the entire continent in the name of the British king. He made no such proclamation at Botany Bay, although he did raise the British flag on the Botany Bay beach.

During our stay in this Harbour, he wrote, *I caused the English Colours to be displayed ashore every day and an inscription to be cut out upon one of the trees near the watering place setting forth the Ship's name, date & C^a.*[9]

Sailing north and charting the east coast of the continent, naming many land points as he progressed, Cook encountered Aboriginal people in various ports of call. His only significant interaction with them, however, was in far north Queensland where the *Endeavour* had to be beached for repairs, after striking the Great Barrier Reef. The ship had struck the reef just before midnight on the night of 11th June 1770 and was almost lost. With a hole in the hull of their ship, the crew threw overboard everything they could, including the ship's heavy cannons, and eventually managed to bring *Endeavour* off the reef, nurse her into shore and beach her at the mouth of a river which Cook later named Endeavour River. For seven weeks, while repairs were made to the ship and while Joseph Banks collected botanical specimens onshore, Cook managed to established some limited level of interaction with the local Guugu Yimithirr people.

By the beginning of August, temporary repairs to *Endeavour* gave Cook sufficient confidence to put to sea again and continue the voyage, albeit it very tentatively. The coastal area of far north Queensland contains many reefs and small islands and Cook sent his pinnace and longboats ahead to feel the way and literally tow *Endeavour* through a maze of islands,

16

reefs and dangerous tidal channels. Cook felt his way through a strait between northernmost tip of what is now Cape York Peninsula and an island which he named Prince of Wales Island. The treacherous strait he named after his ship, Endeavour Strait.

On 21st August 1770, *Endeavour* rounded the northernmost point of the Australian continent and turned westward into another dangerous channel which would later be named the Torres Strait. On this same day, Cook wrote in his journal:

> *The point of the Main*[land] *which forms one side of the passage before mentioned and which is the Northern promontory of this country I have named York Cape in honour of His late Royal Highness the Duke of York.*[10] (Word in brackets added by the author for clarification.)

The name York Cape would later become Cape York.

Some fifteen miles southwest of Cape York, Cook landed on a small island where he climbed the highest hill and looked westward through his telescope, searching for a passage through the islands. The view showed a clear passage to the west and Cook determined there would be no further reason for him to make landings on the New Holland continent. Cook named that small island Possession Island and, before returning to his ship, it was there on that hill that he claimed the entire eastern half of the New Holland continent in the name of the British King.

Back on board *Endeavour*, he would write in his journal:

> *Having satisfied myself of the great Probability of a Passage, thro' which I intend going with the Ship and therefore may land no more upon this Eastern coast of New Holland and on the Western side I can make no new discovery, the honour of which belongs to the Dutch Navigators, but the Eastern Coast from the*

Latitude of 38° South down to this place I am confident was never seen or visited by any European before.[11]…

Notwithstanding, I had in the Name of his Majesty taken possession of several places upon this coast I now once more hoisted English Colours and in the Name of His Majesty King George the Third took possession of the whole Eastern Coast from the above Latitude down to this place by the Name of New South Wales together with all the Bays, Harbours, Rivers and Islands situate upon the said coast after which we fired three Volleys of small Arms which were answered by the like number from the Ship.[12]

He made no reference whatsoever to the Indigenous people of the land he was claiming. To "take possession" of a land which he knew to be populated by Indigenous people was an audacious act and should, at the very least, have recognised the existing inhabitants as the owners and custodians of the land. Naming the land he had encountered "New South Wales" was an effort to separate the land which he had now claimed for the British King from any Dutch interest in the land they had long called New Holland.

From Possession Island, Cook sailed *Endeavour* westward, headed for Batavia, present day Jakarta, in the Dutch East Indies where he would make more permanent repairs to his ship. He would never return to New South Wales but, as he sailed away, he wrote a telling observation about the people he had encountered there:

From what I have said of the Natives of New Holland they may appear to some to be the most wretched people upon Earth, but in reality they are far more happier than we Europeans; being wholly unacquainted not only with the superfluous but the necessary conveniences so much sought after in Europe, they are happy in not knowing the use of them. They live in a Tranquillity which is not disturbed by the Inequality of Condition. The Earth and sea of

*their own accord furnishes them with all things necessary for life,
they covet not magnificent houses, household-stuff etc, they live in a
warm and fine climate and enjoy a very wholesome air, so that they
have very little need of clothing and this they seem to be fully
sencible* [sic] *of, for many to whom we gave cloth etc to, left it
carelessly on the sea beach and in the woods as a thing they had no
manner of use for. In short they seemed to set no value upon
anything we gave them, nor would they ever part with anything of
their own for any one article we could offer them; this in my opinion
argues that they think themselves provided with all the necessarys*
[sic] *of life and that they have no superfluities.* [13]

Therein, lies the very genesis of what, eighteen years
later, would be called "the native problem", which the invaders
would fail to come to grips with except by force of arms. They
would be faced with what perhaps could be called a clash of
cultures but what, essentially, was a clash of values.

As Cook had quite correctly written: *"They live in a
Tranquillity which is not disturbed by the Inequality of Condition"* and
"In short they seemed to set no value upon anything we gave them."

The Indigenous peoples clearly, placed no value on
anything that the Europeans had to offer. They were simply
annoyed that their lifestyle had been disturbed which, again,
was indicative of different values. They were happy and
content living as they did and, as Cook had written, they
believed they had been provided with all the necessities of life.
They wanted nothing other than for the men in their tall ship
to be gone.

That is not to say that they valued nothing. Clearly, they
did. They valued their family structures, their isolation and
their inalienable right to just go on living in their "tranquillity",
to use Cook's word. Most of all, they valued their land – their
relationships and obligations to it. Cook had recognised that
too when he wrote: *"the Earth and sea of their own accord furnishes*

them with all things necessary for life". They were, in effect, People of the Land, and Cook knew it, notwithstanding his limited interaction with them.

Of course, when the European colonists came back with their tall ships eighteen years later, that land and its waters would be at the very centre of conflicts between black and white. Land – the thing the Aboriginals valued above all else and upon which their very survival depended, and which the colonists wanted, above all else, to take from them.

So, where does James Cook fit into this conflict between black and white Australians? Firstly, it is important to recognise that Cook never claimed to have "discovered" Australia, although he did claim to be the first European to sight the east coast of the continent. The words on his statue in Sydney's Hyde Park have been put into his mouth by those who erected the statue. The Australian continent has a long and rich Indigenous history. The Aboriginal peoples, the First Peoples of this land, were among the first to leave Africa and to travel down the coast of India and across the land bridge from Asia before arriving in this country. *They* were the true discoverers of Australia.

As Cook sailed *Endeavour* up the east coast of New Holland, his primary focus was to determine whether the land was occupied and, crucially, if so, the nature of that occupation.

It was obviously occupied, although to what extent remained unclear. Yet, to the British, occupation of the land did not necessarily equate to ownership. The questions which the British believed would determine their right to claim the land as their own included whether the inhabitants of the land were static dwellers or whether they were largely nomadic – and Cook had no idea of the answer to that question. Further

20

questions were whether the inhabitants of the land had built homes, even cities, and whether they had cultivated the land for agrarian purposes. Also, had they developed social and political structures? Were they engaged in exploiting the natural resources of the land? As far as Cook and Banks could see from their very limited contact, the answer to all those questions was "No".

The negative answer to those questions meant to the British that the inhabitants of the land were not "owners" of the land and, thus, the land belonged to nobody – it was *terra-nullius*. It meant that, Cook having claimed the land in the name of the British King, they could establish a colony there that would henceforth be considered their own. There would be no cause to seek a treaty with the inhabitants or persuade them to cede sovereignty of the land because they were not "owners" of the land.

Cook was a man of his times, from all accounts an able explorer, a navigator and an honourable man. Yet he was operating on the premise that those questions to which he had answered "No" were legitimate questions that would and should decide Britain's right to claim the land as their own. It may, therefore, be said that Cook was an enabler – he enabled those who would follow in his path.

Many if not all other European powers of the eighteenth century would have shared Cook's faith in the legitimacy of those questions and in the right of the British to make the land their own. Times change and we, or at least some of us, change with it and can only shake our heads and roll our eyes at the concept of *terra-nullius*.

There is no escaping the fact that Cook did go on to claim the entire eastern half of Australia in the name of King George III, thereby giving the British Crown, in their eyes, exclusive rights to negotiate future settlement sites via treaty with the Indigenous peoples – something that never happened. To have claimed the land for the British King, in the presence of ongoing and longstanding pre-occupation, would be seen, today, as an audacious act and as the political prelude to an act of invasion.

2

INVASION DAY
26th January 1788

History, it is said, is written by the victors. Yet, the vanquished have a story to tell too. In Australia, the victors consider 26th January to be a day of celebration commemorating the founding of the colony of New South Wales, which ultimately led to the establishment of a new, young nation. "Australia Day", they call that day and they celebrate with fireworks, flag-waving, the granting of Australia Day honours to those deemed worthy, the singing of the national anthem and the announcement of "Australian of the Year", all wrapped up in a public holiday, barbeques, beach parties and varying levels of intoxication. There are speeches by the Governor-General speaking on behalf of the British King, by politicians and by state governors. Local mayors give addresses at citizenship ceremonies where migrants to this land take an oath of allegiance to the British King and to "his heirs and successors", thus becoming Australian citizens. There are free concerts in city parks, ferry races on Sydney Harbour as Air Force jets fly overhead and the victors drive around showing off their classic but noisy Holden Torana cars sporting small Australian flags. There are twenty-one-gun salutes, and Royal Australian Navy vessels appear in ports around the country.

Some Indigenous people join the celebrations, though often in a more sombre and subdued manner. There are "Welcome to Country" ceremonies, smoking ceremonies and Aboriginal dances accompanied by the haunting sound of the didgeridoo. In general, though, the vanquished abhor that day – the day the white Europeans came in their tall ships and stole their land.

"Invasion Day", they call that day and they weep, remembering the dispossession of their land, the stealing of their women and their children, the massacres and the ongoing estrangement of many First Nations Peoples from mainstream society – relegated to the status of fringe-dwellers on what used to be their own land. Many engage in noisy protest gatherings and marches, wanting the celebrating victors to pause on that day to remember the plight of the vanquished. "Always Was, Always Will Be, Aboriginal Land", they chant. Many of them become angry and express their anger in various ways, something that will be explored later in this story. They have just cause for their weeping and anger.

Indigenous activist groups and their supporters, a growing number of which are white Australians, campaign for the abolition of Australia Day, or at least for a change of date for that celebration. Yet, Prime Ministers from both sides of the political divide have refused to consider changing the date. They realise changing the date may well result in a backlash at the ballot box when next they must face the electorate. Doing nothing is the safer political option.

"Australians all let us rejoice, for we are one and free," the victors sing – the first words of the Australian National Anthem. Until 1st January 2021, those words were "for we are *young* and free". The change was made in an attempt to be more inclusive, in particular to be inclusive of Indigenous Australians. Yet, it was a symbolic change only for we are not "one and free". There is no evidence that the changed words made the slightest change to the consciousness of either Indigenous or white Australians and, essentially, we remain as divided as we have been since 26th January 1788.

Arthur Phillip sailed from Portsmouth, England, on Sunday 13th May 1787 and, eight and a half months later, arrived at Botany Bay with the vanguard of the fleet on 18th January 1788. The remainder of the fleet, led by *HMS Sirius*, arrived two days later on 21st January 1788.

One can only wonder at the thoughts occupying the minds of the Eora people who stood on the shores of Botany Bay and watched the tall ships sail into their bay, seemingly carried by low-lying white clouds, until the clouds collapsed in on themselves and the tall ships slowed to a halt half a mile offshore. Some of the elders amongst the natives may have remembered another ship carried by those white clouds which had briefly visited their land almost twenty years earlier. Yet, on that occasion there had been only one ship, and it had left their shores after only a short sojourn. Perhaps the same would happen on this occasion. Yet there may also have been some foreboding, especially amongst the elders that, unlike a single ship, the arrival of such a large fleet could be a portent of a coming storm.

The thoughts occupying the minds of the white skinned people on board the tall ships are easier to interpret. They had sailed eight and a half months to this place with one purpose in mind – to establish a British colony on these shores. They stood on the decks of the tall ships, beholding their new land. They had come to stay and to rule.

One of those standing on board a transport ship of the fleet was thirty-year-old Lieutenant-Captain Watkin Tench, part of the marine detachment under Major Robert Ross. Tench had served with the British Marine Corps in the American War of Independence, during which time he spent several months as a prisoner of the American forces. In 1786, with the American war well and truly in the past, Tench volunteered for a three-year tour of duty with the marines who would be sent to Botany Bay as part of the First Fleet. Before leaving England, Tench came to an agreement with Debretts of London, to publish his journal describing the journey to New Holland and the first colony at Botany Bay. Concerning Arthur Phillip's first steps ashore, at Botany Bay, Tench would write:

> *We found the natives tolerably numerous as we advanced up the river, and even at the harbour's mouth we had reason to conclude the country more populous than Mr Cook thought it. For on the Supply's arrival in the bay* [Botany Bay] *on the 18th of the month they assembled on the beach of the south shore to the number of not less than forty persons, shouting and making many uncouth signs and gestures. This appearance whetted curiosity to its utmost, but as prudence forbade a few people to venture wantonly among so great a number, and a party of only six men was observed on the north shore, the governor immediately proceeded to land on that side in order to take possession of this new territory and bring about an intercourse between its new and old masters.*[22] (Words in brackets added by the author for clarification.)

Tench's book is interesting and is written in a style that makes easy reading. In places, however, his writing reflects a sense of European superiority over more primitive people – the same sense of superiority as had been evident in the instructions to Phillip from the British government. This attitude is reflected in the above quote where Tench spoke of intentions to *"take possession of this new territory"* and of *"its new and old masters"*, clear evidence that the colonists came with the intention to rule over the Indigenous people.

By 24th January 1788, however, Phillip had decided that Botany Bay was not a suitable place for the establishment of a new colony and, after some short exploration, he settled on a site only twenty miles north – a harbour which James Cook had named Port Jackson. It would in later times be more commonly known as Sydney Harbour. On 26th January 1788, Phillip, on *HMS Supply*, led the fleet to a place near the western extremity of the harbour to a site he had named Sydney Cove – and there he proclaimed the founding of the Colony of New South Wales, no doubt watched by a relatively small gathering of Indigenous men who wondered at the strange actions of the men from the tall ships. They would have wondered even further had they been able to understand Phillip's words and the true significance of the act.

Effectively, the British had come ashore and raised a strange piece of red, white and blue fabric to the top of a pole which they had erected on the sandy shore. Then, as the natives watched, the men from the tall ships appeared to act in deference to that piece of fabric, almost as if it were an object of worship. Standing around that pole as the strange piece of fabric fluttered in the sea breeze, their leader and spokesman had then declared that the land and everything within it, including the Indigenous people, were now owned and ruled by a king who lived on the other side of the world. One cannot help but wonder at the exchange that may have taken place had the colonists and the Indigenous people shared a common language that allowed the Indigenous watchers to understand the impudence and effrontery of Phillip's claim. The act was staggering in its audacity, it displayed an arrogant right-to-rule posture, and the colonists should not have been surprised, though they were, when the Indigenous people began to resist.

Convicts gradually disembarked from the transport ships over a period of about ten days. Trees were felled to clear a small area for the settlement, tents were erected, timber and stone houses and stores began to be constructed. The local Indigenous people could only watch as the area they called Warrane began to change indelibly.

It would not be until mid-July of that year, 1788, that the last of the fleet's transport ships would set sail and return to England, leaving at Sydney Cove only the two ships of the Royal Navy, *HMS Sirius* and *HMS Supply*. Also left behind on the shores of Sydney Cove were approximately 1,250 souls, around 700 of whom were convicts.

The invasion had commenced.

3

ESTABLISHING A BEACHHEAD
1788 – 1792

When any invading force establishes itself on invaded territory, even if it be only a foothold, the thing that is then most desired by the commanding officer of that force is compliance and a state of peaceful relations with the vanquished inhabitants, in order that the invaders can get on with consolidating their presence as the governing force.

With that in mind, Arthur Phillip turned his mind to his instructions from the Colonial Office that he *"endeavour by every possible means to open an Intercourse with the Natives and to conciliate their affections"*. The problem was that an intercourse takes two parties and the Indigenous people around Sydney Cove, Warrane as they called it, were not interested in establishing friendly relations with the newcomers. What they *were* interested in was attacking unarmed convicts and, on occasions, even armed marines whenever they ventured beyond the Sydney settlement and trespassed on Eora land, for even the Eora themselves would not enter the land of other clans without permission. To do so invited violent retaliation.

To put the natives in their place and enforce the British rights to passage, Phillip sent two armed expeditions to Botany Bay in October 1788 to intimidate the Eora by showing the might of British arms. The purpose of these two expeditions, Judge Advocate David Collins would write, was to show the Eora *"that their late acts of violence would neither intimidate nor prevent us from moving beyond the settlement whenever occasion required it."*[23]

Further impeding Phillip's endeavours to establish relations of any kind with the Eora people was the fact that he erroneously thought them all to be one people. Eora meant, simply, "people". It would be some time before Lieutenant William Dawes, the colony's resident astronomer and amateur linguist, determined that the Eora were comprised of different clans or social gatherings based on extended family relationships. In the Botany Bay-Port Jackson area alone, there may have been up to forty different clans in which the members were all related to one another. Some relationships between the clans existed, for clan members were not permitted to marry within their clan. When marriage occurred, the woman became part of the man's clan and, though the woman was incorporated into the man's clan in a most bizarre and forceful manner, she brought with her the language and knowledge of Country from her own clan. David Collins describes this courtship and marriage ritual in vivid detail:

> *These unfortunate victims of lust and cruelty (it will admit of no better term) are, it is believed, always selected from the women of a different tribe from that of the males, (for they ought not to be dignified with the title of men) and with whom they are at enmity. Secrecy is necessarily observed, and the poor wretch is stolen upon in the absence of her protectors. Being first stupefied with blows, inflicted with clubs or wooden swords, on the head, back, and shoulders, every one of which is followed by a stream of blood, she is then dragged through the woods by one arm, with a perseverance and violence that it might be supposed would displace it from its socket. The lover, or rather the ravisher, is regardless of the stones or broken pieces of trees which may lie in his route, being anxious only to convey his prize, in safety, to his own party, where a scene ensues too shocking to relate. This outrage is not resented by the relations of the female, who only retaliate by a similar outrage when they find an opportunity. This is so constantly the practice among them, that even the children make it a play-game or exercise. The women thus ravished become their wives and are incorporated into the tribes to which their husbands belong.*[24]

Thus, it was not unusual for members of one clan to know the language of other clans and, because of the inter-clan relationships formed through marriage, they were able to engage in hunting, fishing and gathering pursuits together, yet they remained separate and distinct clans. Eora was a term used collectively for the various native clans living around the Port Jackson area – the Gadigal, Wangal, Gameragal, Baramadigal and Warramadigal. And, in early 1788, the Eora already had a name for the newcomers – Berewalgal – "the people of the clouds". The suffix "gal", William Dawes had established meant "clan" or "nation".

The Berewalgal, under Phillip's instructions, attempted to establish a relationship with the Eora through the giving of gifts and apparent friendly acts, even dancing. Yet, at the same time, the colonists were intent upon putting the Eora in their place and convincing them that they were a primitive and backward race who would be unable to prevail in any act of armed conflict against them. Part of this included displaying to the Eora the superiority of modern European weaponry. Lieutenant Watkin Tench wrote of this in his journal:

> *Our first object was to win their affections, and our next was to convince them of the superiority we possessed: for without the latter, the former we knew would be of little importance. So, they fired the muskets over the heads of the Eora and shot musket balls right through their wooden shields.*[25]

When Tench wrote of *"the superiority we possessed"* he may have been thinking in terms of the superior weapons or he may have been thinking of a general superiority in every way – the two concepts may have been inseparable in his mind. In any event, the demonstration of musket balls being fired through their shields was not lost on the Eora who, thereafter, avoided the settlement at Sydney Cove, thus leaving Phillip with virtually no opportunities to establish his intercourse with them. Indeed, the display by the colonists of the superiority of their weapons seems a counterproductive way to *"conciliate their affections".* Phillip had hoped that Eora family groups would come into the settlement and live there, giving the colonists opportunities to learn more about them, and particularly about how numerous they were, but by now the Eora were very wary of the Berewalgal and their weapons.

The ensuing uneasy standoff frustrated Phillip who then embarked upon a new strategy for establishing friendly relations with the Eora – he would capture some native warriors, hold them in irons at Government House and force them to be his friends. In the twenty-first century we shake our heads and ask, "What was the man thinking?" Yet his actions displayed not only his mounting frustration but also his innate sense of superiority over the Indigenous people.

Knowing that the Eora were numerous in an area just inside the North Head of Port Jackson, an area that would later be named Manly Cove, Phillip dispatched marines in longboats with orders to capture some Eora warriors. They captured only one – a young man named Arabanoo, who was then detained in irons at Government House.

The Hungry Years

With no supply ships expected from England for at least two years, successful production of grain and vegetables was essential if the colony was not to starve. In an endeavour to provide the required agricultural produce, the cove to the east of Sydney Cove had been named Farm Cove where some ten acres had been sown with maize and vegetables. Yet the acreage at Farm Cove produced very little food. The soil there, and everywhere around Sydney Cove, was poor and unsuitable for farming endeavours. Exacerbating the problem was the fact that almost all convicts had been taken from the streets of

London and from other British cities and had little or no knowledge of farming practices.

Phillip knew the colony's supplies of food would last little more than a year, yet he could see that it would take much longer than that for the colony to become self-sufficient. Day by day, supplies of food diminished, rations were reduced to what Phillip considered a minimal level, then reduced again, and a general state of malaise and despair embraced Sydney Cove. As the colonists waited and hoped for much needed provisions from England, work at the settlement petered away and then ceased. Phillip, wanting to maintain a sense of purpose, had done his best to maintain construction work in the settlement, but starving men cannot work. Convicts, male and female, shuffled about the settlement, seemingly devoid of hope and interest in life, their feet dragging desultorily in the sandy dust of Sydney Cove until instinctively returning to their huts to sleep or to die. Marines wandered about aimlessly, not wasting efforts on conversation with convicts other than when disagreements turned into arguments and fights. Every person, including the Governor, was living on less than half rations, and those rations were being drawn from rotting salted pork that was more than two years old, and weevil-ridden flour. A state of near starvation sapped not only the energy of all at Sydney Cove, but also their hope, their morale, and their confidence in the future. The convicts believed they had not only been exiled, but forgotten, abandoned, and left to starve. The situation became so dire that at the beginning of October 1788, Arthur Phillip dispatched *HMS Sirius* to Cape Town, with orders to buy much needed food for the colony. Phillip anticipated a return voyage of about eight months and, until *Sirius* arrived back at Sydney Cove, the colonists and the convicts would barely avoid starvation.

Sirius left Port Jackson under the command of Captain John Hunter on 2nd October 1788. From Sydney, Hunter chose the faster but more perilous route, sailing east using the strong westerly winds known as the 'Roaring Forties' and rounding Cape Horn, before continuing on to the Cape of Good Hope. After loading at Cape Town, he set sail eastward again, arriving back in Port Jackson on 8th May 1789. Hunter had driven *Sirius* hard and she had circumnavigated the globe in a voyage of seven months, including several weeks of loading time at the Cape. Yet, Arthur Phillip was only too aware that, even these extra supplies, whilst they might save the colony for a time, were not adequate to ensure long term survival. He calculated that, if supplied at the level of full rations, the new provisions would last only an extra four months, so everyone within the colony, bound and free, including the Governor himself, remained on half rations.

Contagion

Soon, Phillip realised that he was dealing not only with the challenge of feeding the colony but also with a deadly epidemic affecting the natives. The Berewalgal had brought much more than their muskets when they came to Sydney Cove – they also brought a myriad of diseases to which the Eora had no natural resistance. In April 1789, quite suddenly they began dying of a terrible illness. Native corpses floated in the turquoise waters of Sydney Cove and, on the foreshores of every bay in the harbour, they were dying in large numbers, their emaciated corpses left on the sandy beaches, on the rocks and amongst the trees. Pus-filled blisters covered every inch of their bodies, making them all but unrecognisable, even to family. The surviving natives, usually respectful about the disposal of their dead, fled into the interior, leaving behind putrid, rotting corpses on the beaches which permeated the settlement with the penetrating silence of death. Phillip took one look at the first corpse he encountered and knew immediately what he was seeing – smallpox.

He knew, also, that they had brought this scourge to New South Wales with them. There had been cases amongst the convicts at the Cape, more than a year and a half earlier. Whether they had brought it with them from England or contracted it at the Cape, Phillip did not know. Yet, those cases at the Cape had been isolated – the men involved had either died or been left behind to die when the fleet sailed from the Cape on 25th November 1787, and there had been no more cases within the white community, either at Sydney Cove, Rose Hill, or Norfolk Island. It was only the natives who were being decimated by the spread of this deadly disease. Empty native canoes were now seen on the harbour, floating desolately and rocked by the small harbour swell or pulled up and abandoned on the beaches. Their owners had either died or escaped to the interior of the colony in a desperate attempt to leave behind the sickness and death which they knew had been visited upon them by the Berewalgal. Only the dead and the dying remained.

When Phillip turned to his Chief Surgeon, John White, and asked why it was only the natives who were afflicted, White looked at him solemnly and explained that, because most of the Europeans had been exposed to the disease in their infancy, they had established a certain level of immunity. The natives had no immunity because the disease had never been known in their country. White went on to advise Phillip that there would likely be other epidemics too – measles, influenza and possibly tuberculosis. Phillip knew and recognised the scars of smallpox that were always left on survivors. He had seen it in England and knew that prior to the outbreak of the epidemic he had seen no sign of it amongst the natives. He readily accepted Surgeon White's assumption that the disease had never been known in this land.

According to colonial estimates at the time, 50% of the Indigenous population of the area were killed by the smallpox epidemic. Contemporary estimates put the total at closer to 70%. One of those afflicted was Phillip's chained friend, Arabanoo, who suddenly fell ill with the disease in mid-May 1789. Living in close proximity with the Berewalgal, as he had, it was only surprising that he had not contracted the dreadful disease earlier. Surgeon White did everything in his powers to save him, but Arabanoo died on 18th May 1789. Over several months, Phillip and Arabanoo had established a growing relationship as each learned a little of the other's language, and the death of his chained friend appears to have caused Phillip some genuine sentiments of grief. He ordered Arabanoo's body to be buried within the gardens of Government House.

It should be acknowledged at this point that some contemporary historians speculate that the deadly smallpox bacteria, variola, had been deliberately released by the colonists in an attempt to exterminate the Indigenous peoples – a form of biological warfare. Vials of smallpox scabs had been brought from England by Surgeon John White believing they could be used for the treatment of settlers should there be an outbreak of smallpox amongst them. There is no record of what happened to those toxic vials after arrival at Sydney Cove. Thus, a deliberate release of the deadly bacteria must remain a possibility, horrendous though it is to the civilised mind. The writings of Phillip, Collins, Hunter and Tench, however, appear to be genuine in the expression of their grief and remorse, thus rendering a deliberate release an unlikely scenario. There is no doubt that the deadly disease had been brought to these shores by the colonists, but it is the opinion of this author that it was an unintended consequence of their invasion of the land rather than a deliberate release.

Towards the end of November 1789, the epidemic appeared to have run its course and natives began returning to their ancestral homelands, their Country around the harbour, though they still avoided the Berewalgal settlement at Sydney Cove.

Phillip knew that, to some extent, his experiment with the capture and holding of Arabanoo had been successful for Arabanoo had provided information that Phillip sought about the natives – their social structure, their customs, their tribal relationships and their numbers. Now with the death of Arabanoo and with the natives still avoiding the settlement at Sydney Cove, Phillip ordered the capture of more native warriors who, like Arabanoo, would be held in chains at Government House. On 25th November 1789, Phillip dispatched marines, again to Manly Cove, under the command of Lieutenant William Bradley, with instructions to capture a number of Eora warriors. Bradley would write at length about this expedition in his unpublished journal:

> *Wednesday, 25th: Governor Phillip judging it necessary that a Native should be taken by force, (no endeavour to persuade them to come among us having succeeded) I was order'd on this service, having the Master, two Petty Officers and a Boats Crew with me in one of the Governor's boats: As we went down the Harbour we got some fish from the boats that lay off the No.Arm* [North Arm] *fishing and proceeded up the Arm in which we saw a great number of Natives on both sides and several landed on the beach at the No.Cove* [North Cove] *hauling their canoes up after them; As we got near the upper part of the No.Cove, we held two large fish up to them and had the good luck to draw two of them away from a very large party by this bait, these People came around the rocks where they left their spears and met us on the beach near the boat and at a distance from their Companions sufficient to promise success without losing any lives, they eagerly*

took the fish, four of the boats crew were kept in the boat which was winded and back'd close to the beach where the two Natives and the rest of our People were, they were dancing together when the Signal was given by me and the two poor devils were seiz'd and handed into the boat in an instant. The Natives who were very numerous all round us, on seeing us seize those two, immediately advanced with their Spears and Clubs, but we were too quick for them, being out of reach before they got to that part of the beach where the boat lay, they were entering on the beach just as everybody was in the boat and as she did not take the ground we pulled immediately out without having occasion to fire a Musquet [sic]; The noise of the Men, Crying and screaming of the Women and Children together with the situation of the two miserable wretches in our possession was really a most distressing scene; they were much terrified, one of them particularly so, the other frequently called out to those on shore apparently very much enraged with them, they followed the boat on both sides as far as the points of the Cove and then Returned to the beach, we saw them take up the two fish which their two unfortunate friends dropt on being seiz'd. On our landing at Sydney Cove, we were met by Nanbarry, the Native boy who was much pleas'd and called them by name Colbey and Bennalon. Colbey we have frequently heard spoken of by the Boy as a great Warrior and a leading Man among them; they were taken to the Governor's House where they were soon met by Abooroo, the Native Girl, she called them by name the same as the boy had done and was quite frantic with Joy; they were assured by these Children that they would be well treated and thereafter allowed to return to their friends, but all that could be said or done was not sufficient to remove the pang which they naturally felt at being torn away from their Friends; or to reconcile them to their situation.[26] (Words in brackets added by the author for clarification.)

It is worth quoting Bradley in full because one of the two captured warriors was a Wangal man, Bennelong, whose story would be an integral part of Berewalgal–Eora interactions during the remainder of Phillip's governorship. The other warrior captured was Colbee, an older and respected man of the Gadigal people who somehow managed to escape Government House within three weeks of his capture.

After the escape of Colbee, Bennelong, perhaps because of his sense of isolation, began responding to the questions of his Berewalgal interrogators. He told them the names, populations and territories of the Eora clans – information which the governor thought most useful though how much of it was truthful and how much was deception on the part of Bennelong was questionable and remains so today.

Lieutenant Watkin Tench was a close observer of Bennelong and perhaps one of his interrogators. Tench wrote of Bennelong:

> *His powers of mind were suddenly far above mediocrity. He acquired knowledge, both of our manners and language far faster than his predecessor* [Arabanoo] *had done. He willingly communicated information, sang, danced and told us all the customs of his country and all the details of his family economy. Love and war seemed his favourite pursuits, in both of which he had suffered severely. His head was disfigured by several scars. A spear had passed through his arm and another through his leg. Half of one of his thumbs was carried away and the mark of a wound appeared on the back of his hand.*[27] (Word in brackets added by the author for clarification.)

Bennelong seemed to be providing the Governor with most of the information he was seeking whilst, at the same time, learning all he could about the Berewalgal, their home country, the power of their marines and their weapons. He dined at the Governor's table, was plied with wine and drank toasts to the health of "The King".

Meanwhile, the settlement at Norfolk Island, where the soil was more fertile and the climate more accommodating, was finding cultivation more successful than at Sydney Cove and was almost self-sufficient. Phillip hoped that, in time, Norfolk would be able to supply excess grain to Sydney Cove, yet he knew he did not have that time. If no ships from England reached Port Jackson soon, they would find only graves and empty buildings when, and if, they eventually arrived. In late-April 1790, Phillip dispatched both *Sirius* and *Supply* to Norfolk Island with large contingents of convicts and marines as part of a dual-purpose strategy – to hopefully increase the amount of food that could be produced on Norfolk and at the same time to lessen demand on the fast-dwindling supplies of food at Sydney Cove. The two ships sailed from Port Jackson in March 1790, leaving behind a population reduced to half that which had arrived in January 1788. *Sirius* was under orders to discharge her passengers at Norfolk quickly and to immediately return to Port Jackson where she would be readied for another mercy mission to procure more provisions.

Disastrous news reached Phillip, early in April 1790, with the return of *HMS Supply*, alone. *HMS Sirius* had been wrecked on the treacherous reef at Slaughter Bay in Norfolk Island on 19th March and would never sail again. Phillip immediately, though with some reluctance, ordered the smaller *HMS Supply* be readied for a voyage to Batavia in the Dutch East Indies with her captain, Lieutenant Henry Ball, instructed to procure there provisions such as she could carry. Ball was also ordered to make every attempt to charter a Dutch ship to carry extra supplies to Sydney Cove. *Supply* set sail from Port Jackson, bound for Batavia with all possible haste on 17th April 1790. The Governor knew he was risking the colony's only vessel and that, even if she made it back safely, the provisions she could bring would stave off starvation for only a few months. Where was the Second Fleet he had been promised? Where were the carpenters, builders and bricklayers he needed to consolidate the settlement he had established? Most urgently, where were the life-enabling and desperately needed supplies and provisions? Had he been betrayed? Had the colony at Sydney Cove been forgotten and abandoned by the home government? The population of the settlement sank further into despair as they watched *Supply* sail towards the Heads and Batavia. They knew she was on an urgent mission to procure supplies that might keep them alive for a few more months. Yet, with the harbour now empty and with no way of reaching out to the outside world, a greater feeling of abandonment further oppressed them.

In April 1790, Governor Phillip, believing his captured friend, Bennelong, could now be trusted, ordered the irons removed from his legs. Bennelong thanked the Governor, stripped off his Berewalgal clothes and fled the settlement, returning to his Country and to his own people. His Country, he knew, had always provided for his needs and for the needs of his people, not always abundantly but always adequately. He knew he would eat better in his Country than he would here in the camp of the Berewalgal who seemed to have been burdened with an illness of the spirit as they waited for the arrival of yet another of those ships carried by low-lying clouds which they believed, or hoped, would bring them food from the land of the King.

Phillip, who thought he had developed something approaching a father-son relationship with Bennelong, was of two minds – he was disappointed, of course, to have lost his friend Bennelong, yet he realised it was one less mouth for him to feed as the colony struggled to survive.

If nothing else, those 'Hungry Years' prevented any significant intrusions into Aboriginal land because, for the time being, Phillip was preoccupied with keeping his small settlements alive, meaning less occasions for conflict with the natives who were still avoiding the settlement of the Berewalgal at Warane. The Governor knew that the long-term survivability of the colony would ultimately depend upon extending the agricultural footprint into the interior, away from Sydney Cove, but that would be in the future – it was not immediately possible. A small settlement had been established at Rose Hill, which soon reverted to its Aboriginal name of Parramatta (the place of the eels), and the settlement there held hopes of more successful cultivation than at Sydney Cove, but not in time to save the colony from starvation. At Sydney Cove, even the thick forest surrounding the settlement which they had worked so hard to establish seemed, to Phillip, to be intent on once again encroaching upon it and reclaiming it as its own.

As the lack of provisions at Sydney Cove became more and more desperate, the Governor looked at the native canoes fishing in the harbour and ordered that all boats in the colony, both government owned and private, were to be constantly engaged in fishing. He also ordered that the best marksmen from amongst the marines were to be engaged in hunting kangaroos and other native animals, with all catches of fish and all animals shot to be requisitioned by the government stores. The fishermen fished day and night, the lamps in their boats bobbing up and down in the small harbour swell. They had varying success, sometimes returning to shore with substantial catches, sometimes with very little or none. Meanwhile, the marines managed to shoot very few animals. These almost desperate efforts by Phillip to feed the settlement, however, had a deleterious effect on the hunting and gathering lifestyle of the natives. The armada of small boats fishing in the harbour made it more difficult for the natives to attract and capture fish while the attempts by the marines to shoot wildlife had the effect of driving kangaroos and other native animals away from the area.

Then, on 3rd June 1790, the *Lady Juliana* reached Port Jackson after a ten month voyage from England, carrying some provisions but also two hundred and twenty-two female convicts who would be an added drain on the already scant provisions. Worse still, they brought devastating news – firstly they told of the loss of the main supply ship, *HMS Guardian*, which should have arrived in Port Jackson five months earlier in February 1790. *Guardian* had hit ice in the Southern Ocean and had almost been lost at sea. She had made it back to Cape Town but would never sail again. A lot of her supplies and all the livestock she had been carrying for the colony in New South Wales, had been lost. The second unwelcome news brought by the *Lady Juliana* was that she was being followed by the transport ships of the Second Fleet which were carrying some much-needed supplies but also over a thousand convicts – and their arrival was imminent. The transport ships, *Neptune*, *Scarborough* and *Surprize*, arrived in Sydney Cove over three days from 26th – 28th June 1790.

The voyage of the three convict transport ships had been hell on earth for the poor wretches they carried. Of the 1,006 convicts who had been embarked at Spithead, 267 convicts had perished during the voyage. On arrival in Sydney Cove, many dead and those close to death were simply cast overboard and floated in the harbour – an obscenity in those turquoise waters. Very few were capable of walking. Cadaverous-looking convicts, near naked, and covered in filth and lice, were carried onto barges and rowed ashore, where they became the responsibility of the Governor.

The settlement's Chaplain, Reverend Dr Richard Johnson, who had arrived with the First Fleet, went aboard *Scarborough* but was so appalled at the sight and the smell on deck that he would not venture below. Johnson would write:

I beheld a sight truly shocking to the feelings of humanity, a great number of them laying, some half, others nearly quite naked, without either bed or bedding, unable to turn or help themselves…

I spoke to them as I passed along, but the smell was so offensive that I could scarcely bear it… The landing of these people was truly affecting and shocking; great numbers were not able to walk, nor to move hand or foot; such were slung over the ship's side in the same manner as they would a cask, a box, or anything of that nature…

Upon their being brought up to the open air some fainted, some died upon deck, and others in the boat before they reached the shore. Some creeped upon their hands and knees, and some were carried upon the backs of others.[28]

During the voyage from England, the convicts had been horrendously treated by the captains and crews of the vessels. With mercenary intent, rations had been withheld from the convicts, enabling the captains to auction unused supplies on arrival at Sydney Cove. Captain William Hill, an officer of the New South Wales Corps who travelled on *Surprize*, would later write home, saying, *"The slave trade is merciful compared with what I have seen in this fleet."*[29]

An incensed Governor Phillip accused the three ship's captains of being murderers and insisted that he would report it to London in his dispatches. But he was left with the fact that his colony had been burdened with more unskilled convicts, most of them weak, emaciated and incapable of work. The already inadequate resources of the settlement would be stretched beyond starvation point.

It was the return of *HMS Supply* to Port Jackson which saved the colony from total starvation. She arrived from Batavia on 19th September 1790, accompanied by the larger Dutch vessel *Waaksamheid* which Lieutenant Ball had chartered to bring more supplies to the starving colony. Ball was promoted and much feted for his efforts. Survival would still be a challenge and all within the colony would continue to exist on half-rations, but a manageable path forward would enable Phillip to extend agricultural development into new areas – into Aboriginal lands.

The arrival of the Second Fleet on 26th – 28th June 1790 saw the marines replaced by the red-coated soldiers of the newly formed New South Wales Corps under the command of Major Francis Grose. Most of the marines would later return to England, though some remained in the colony and were given land grants by the Governor, and a few were incorporated into the Corps. The Corps were far from an efficient, trustworthy and loyal group of soldiers – many were military deserters and civilian lawbreakers who had been given the choice of prison in England or service with the New South Wales Corps. Had the Home Office intended to establish a dishonest, exploitative and oppressive force, they could hardly have done better.

Ever anxious to renew his association with Bennelong, Phillip ordered the officers of the Corps to be constantly on the lookout for him. He did not realise that Bennelong, too, wanted his association with the Governor to be renewed. Bennelong was now the Eora's most knowledgeable warrior about the intent and capabilities of the Berewalgal – knowledge, combined with a certain level of subterfuge, that made him well suited to be something of an ambassador for his people. Yet, first there were some scores to be settled. By being abducted and held captive, Colbee and Bennelong had been wronged, and for such an offence Aboriginal law demanded payback.

On 7ᵗʰ September 1790 a party of Corps soldiers came upon a large gathering of Eora partying on a dead whale beached at Manly Cove. Amongst them was Bennelong who sent an invitation with the soldiers for the Governor to join him at Manly. Phillip received this invitation as welcome news and departed for Manly as soon as it was reported to him. At Manly, Phillip was lured away from his accompanying soldiers and found himself amongst the trees surrounded by Eora warriors. Bennelong, by all accounts, informed Phillip that payback justice was about to be administered – Phillip would be ceremonially speared but he would not be killed. In retrospect, it was a remarkable moment in the history of white interactions with the Indigenous peoples of this land – a young Wangal warrior held in his hands the very life of the King's representative in his land – the same King to whom he had drunk many toasts. Immediately, one of the other warriors launched a spear that struck Phillip in the shoulder. Clearly, had they wished, the warriors could have killed Phillip at that moment, but the spear they had used was not a death spear, and Phillip would soon recover. It seems Phillip understood the reason for the spearing for he ordered his troops not to retaliate and that no subsequent action be taken over the incident.

With the dispensing of payback justice, Bennelong agreed to return to the settlement at Sydney Cove but not in chains and not as a captive at Government House. He declared that he would come and go from Sydney Cove as he pleased and asked Phillip to have a stone house built to accommodate himself and his family during their regular visits to the settlement. Phillip acquiesced, and a stone house was built for Bennelong on a headland on the shores of Sydney Cove. The site is now known as Bennelong Point and is home to the Sydney Opera House.

Phillip and Bennelong developed a deep, personal relationship which caused Watkin Tench to write that Bennelong called Phillip affectionately "Beenèna" (father), while Phillip called him "Doorow" (son):

> *Although I call him only Baneelon, he had besides several appellations; and for a while he chose to be distinguished by that of Wo-lar-a-war-ee. Again, as a mark of affection and respect to the governor, he conferred on him the name of Wolarawaree, and sometimes called him Been-en-a (father); adopting to himself the name of governor. This interchange we found is a constant symbol of friendship amongst them.* [30]

Bennelong's relationship with the Governor developed into that of a quasi-diplomat for his people, which saw him bring to the Governor's attention complaints against the British by the Eora people – complaints that the Governor occasionally accepted and acted upon. In this role, Bennelong's influence and standing was enhanced amongst both the British and the Eora. An increasing number of Eora families entered the settlement, encouraged by the presence of Bennelong and, for a time, the two races lived together peacefully and with a level of mutual curiosity and guarded friendship. It would not last.

Phillip and the Corps commanders now expected the Eora would submit to British law, not only within the Sydney Cove settlement but throughout the colony. It was a naive assumption which failed to take into account fundamental aspects of Eora society. The first cause of ongoing conflict arose from the fact that the Eora, too, had their own system of laws, underpinned by the practice of payback justice. Just as the Berewalgal attempted to extend their law to the Indigenous people, so the Eora would engage payback justice against the Berewalgal when Aboriginal law was transgressed.

Both parties, too, had strategic policies which were diametrically opposed to each other. The British policy was to extend white settlement outwards from Sydney Cove to areas like Parramatta, the Hawkesbury and ultimately throughout the entire country. Phillip knew this was essential if the colony was to survive. The entire territory had been claimed for the British king and the settlement could only survive by extending its agricultural footprint and using the resources of the wider region. Phillip was determined to enforce British policy and to send his Corps soldiers, farmers and settlers wherever he wished. Eora policy sought to contain the Berewalgal to the area they called Warrane, Sydney Cove. Berewalgal farmers, settlers, fishermen and soldiers of the Corps who ventured out of Warrane were viewed by the Eora as trespassers or invaders on Eora land and had to be resisted, often violently.

October 1790 saw a complaint brought by an emissary of the native people living in the Paramatta area. An old man, Maugoran, a Burramattegal elder, came to Government House to respectfully deliver a protest directly to the Governor. The message he brought to Phillip was that the people around Parramatta were very angry at the invasion of their county and that they were being denied access to their staple food sources. Phillip listened courteously and made record of the complaint, writing *"Certain it is that wherever our colonists fix themselves, the natives are obliged to leave that country."* [31]

The Bidjigal clan, living around the area of Botany Bay, were part of the Eora nation but, according to Bennelong, were enemies of his own clan, the Wangal. At this point, Bennelong's story begins to be shrouded in suspected, though unproven, craftiness and duplicity. A Bidjigal warrior, supposedly an enemy of the Wangal, became a regular visitor to Bennelong's house in the settlement. His name was

Pemulwuy, a warrior who would go on to become perhaps the most infamous and feared Aboriginal resistance fighter in the colonial era. Born around 1750 and living in the area of Botany Bay, it is more than likely that Pemulwuy may have seen the *Endeavour* of Captain James Cook carried into the bay by the low-lying white clouds on 29th April 1770 when he would have been about twenty years of age. When the men in their tall ships came back eighteen years later, Pemulwuy was determined to resist the invasion of his Country. Bennelong and Pemulwuy had one shared passion – an intense abhorrence to the Governor's personal game shooter, convict John McIntyre. McIntyre was feared and hated by the Eora people because of his violence towards the Eora, particularly towards their women, and payback was overdue.

In late-November and into early-December 1790, Pemulwuy spent almost two weeks with Bennelong and Colbee at Bennelong's house in the Sydney settlement. Shortly thereafter, on 10th December 1790, Pemulwuy confronted game shooter John McIntyre in the bush near the mouth of the Cooks River in the Botany Bay area, homeland to his Bidjigal clan. McIntyre was fatally speared by Pemulwuy, though he lingered and suffered an agonising death before finally succumbing to his wound on 22nd December. Concerning this incident, Judge Advocate David Collins would write:

> *This man had been suspected of having wantonly killed or wounded several of the natives in the course of his excursions after game; but he steadily denied, from the time he was brought in, to his last moment of life, having ever fired at them but once, and then only in defence of his own life, which he thought in danger.*[32]

Notwithstanding McIntyre's protestations of innocence, the attack by Pemulwuy appears to have been a payback response to his perceived crimes against the Eora people.

On the day of the attack on McIntyre, Bennelong and Colbee made themselves conspicuously present within the Parramatta settlement – they had an alibi, but it is reasonable to suspect that Bennelong and Colbee had colluded with Pemulwuy to kill McIntyre for Bennelong, in particular, hated McIntyre with a passion. Governor Phillip, too, may have suspected Bennelong's involvement in the killing of McIntyre for his senior officers had advised him that Bennelong was a man of cunning duplicity. It was not something Phillip wanted to believe about Bennelong, but his suspicions were being aroused.

Phillip was incensed by the killing of McIntyre and saw it as a betrayal of the agreement that he thought he had with the Eora for peaceful relations. When McIntyre was speared and brought into the settlement at Sydney Cove, Phillip changed from a man seeking peace and good relations with the Eora to one intent on displaying the might of the British forces and on inflicting absolute terror upon them. He ordered Lieutenant Watkin Tench to lead a party of fifty red-coated soldiers with muskets and bayonets into the Botany Bay area to show once and for all that Aboriginal violence against the white colonists would not be tolerated.

It is the nature of the specific instructions given to Tench which still horrifies historians today. Tench was ordered to kill and decapitate ten Eora warriors – any ten would do. The party was equipped with hatchets for chopping and with bags to carry the heads back to Sydney Cove. He was also ordered to capture two Eora men – again, any two would do – and bring them back to Sydney for public execution.

Tench, himself, was horrified at these orders and managed to convince Phillip that they should be moderated.

50

Ultimately, the revised orders called for the capture of six Eora who were to be brought to Sydney Cove where three of them would be hanged. All of this, according to Tench was intended *"to infuse a universal terror which might operate to prevent further mischief."*[33]

Lieutenant William Dawes was ordered to accompany Tench and his troops on this mission. It is worth noting that both Dawes and Tench are considered by many contemporary commentators and historians to have been men sympathetic to the Indigenous cause. Dawes at first had refused to take part in the mission and would later be repatriated to England because of his outspoken condemnation of Phillip. Dawes had declared that, should he be given such orders again, he would refuse to obey.

Phillip's orders to Tench were totally incompatible with British law, even that of the eighteenth century. To apply collective responsibility and guilt, especially involving death sentences, indiscriminately to a group of innocent people because of what one person had done violates any sense of civilised law. The original order to decapitate people, be they dead or alive, was an order for an abhorrent and illegal act. By the very nature of his orders, Phillip had crossed the line from respected public administrator to would-be mass murderer.

It is pertinent, too, to ask what rights the Aboriginal people were entitled to under British law. With the claiming of the territory and all within it as "British Property", owned by the British Crown, the Indigenous people had been declared to be British subjects. Either they were and are British subjects entitled to the protection of British law or they were and are foreign enemies. They could not be both. Even if it could be argued that the territory was a "war zone", that there existed some kind of civil war, an act of mass decapitation would clearly have been considered a war crime.

It has been reported that Phillip was being pressured to supply Aboriginal skulls to Sir Joseph Banks in England who had promised them to medical professor Johann Fredrich Blumenbach at the University of Göttingen. This may explain but not excuse the decapitation order.

To the extent that Phillip can escape utter condemnation for his illegal orders, which seems incredulous to this writer, he can do so only because the mission of Tench and his party was an abject failure. One week after the spearing of McIntyre, Tench marched his red-coated soldiers from Sydney towards the southwest of Botany Bay and then followed the Georges River to the district around modern-day Liverpool. Tench would later report that, during that time, they did not see a single native person. He then led his party back towards Botany Bay where, near the Cooks River, they sighted and tried unsuccessfully to capture a small group of Aboriginal people. They later found another small group on the south shore of Cooks River, but the Aboriginals quickly took to their canoes and paddled across the river to safety. Exhausted and frustrated, Tench then led his dispirited party back to Sydney Cove. They had not captured or killed a single native.

Angered by the failure of the Tench expedition, Phillip ordered them out again on 22nd December. The date is significant because it was on that day that McIntyre finally succumbed to his spear wound and died. The death of McIntyre on that day may have been instrumental in Phillip's decision to send the troops out again. On the second occasion, the party departed Sydney at sunset on 22nd December, with the intent to make a surprise attack before dawn, by which strategy they hoped to arrest or kill the Eora while they slept in their camp. Their objective was a known Aboriginal camp on the banks of the Cooks River but, when the party arrived there in the pre-dawn hours, the camp was deserted and clearly had been so for several days. It seemed the Aboriginals who usually lived at that camp had been forewarned, perhaps by Bennelong. Tench reported that he gave up after dawn and marched the soldiers back to Sydney Cove. Again, they had failed to arrest or kill a single native. Reading Tench's account of this expedition it is difficult to escape the conclusion that he was making little real effort to fulfil his mission.[34]

Frustrated, Phillip now embarked on a new tactic – he would banish all Aboriginal people from settlement areas until such time as they gave up their leader, Pemulwuy. Yet, the Eora would not give up Pemulwuy.

All the while, the colony was expanding further and further into Aboriginal land. Phillip's primary goal was to establish a self-sufficient colony, one in which emancipated convicts were to be given land and everything they needed to become successful famers producing food for the colony.

With that objective in mind, Phillip needed to find arable land where crops could be successfully cultivated on small farms carved out of the bush by convicts who had served their time. Farms were establish in increasing numbers on Aboriginal land at places like Prospect Hill, Rose Hill, Parramatta and The Ponds. Land was the key to the survival and expansion of the colony – land taken from Aboriginal people. Phillip knew that expanding the agricultural areas, critical for the colony's survival, meant dispossessing the Aboriginals of their land and their food sources, yet that was his mission – to build an agrarian-based, self-sustaining colony. He knew, too, that the Aboriginal people would resist further encroachment on their land and, to meet that resistance, he armed the settlers with muskets.

Expansion of the government farm at Parramatta took up a huge parcel of land on the banks of the Parramatta River, denying the Burramattegal people access to water and especially to the eels that they caught in the river and the extensive yam beds, a primary food source for them. The government farm and the accompanying settlement at Parramatta was the first large-scale invasion of the land mass beyond Sydney Cove and it was well defended by the Corps. In an attempt to stop the encroachment of Berewalgal farms on Aboriginal land, the Bidjigal warrior Pemulwuy, the same Pemulwuy who had killed the Governor's game shooter back in 1790, now led a number of raids on white outpost settlements. The first raid was launched at Prospect in May 1792. Pemulwuy knew that the colony was short of food so he burned their crops and attacked farmers isolated in their fields as well as travellers on the road. He and his band of warriors killed the settlers' livestock and raided their houses, plundering all they could before setting the house alight. It was the start of a twelve-year guerrilla war, really a series of wars that would become known as "The Frontier Wars." In subsequent years, however, and even during the years of The Frontier Wars, some settlers befriended local Aboriginals and found ways to co-exist. It was the exception rather than the rule.

By late-1792, Arthur Phillip had spent five years building a colony centred on the place where he had stepped ashore and raised the British flag. The colony, despite Aboriginal resistance, was now spreading beyond Sydney Cove and Parramatta, with pockets of farmland popping up in outlying localities. But it had taken a toll on his health. For more than three years he had suffered periodic but intense and debilitating pain in his side, thought to have been caused by kidney stones. He would gain temporary relief when stones were passed, only to have the pain return when new stones formed. His workload, and particularly his engagement in explorative work into the interior and into the area north of Port Jackson, resulted in extended periods of dehydration — the primary cause of kidney stones. It may also be that at times it impaired his judgement – people who are ill and in significant pain sometimes make rash and aberrant decisions, and kidney stones can cause very severe pain indeed. Thus, Phillip's ordering of Watkin Tench to kill and decapitate natives following the killing of his game shooter, John McIntyre, may possibly have been impaired by pain and illness and may be the reason Phillip readily acquiesced when Tench pleaded for less severe orders. This, of course, is pure speculation and is not meant to expunge those horrific orders from Phillip's history.

Building a colony on foreign shores had been a struggle for Phillip, physically and emotionally, and it may also be that he was growing weary of the fight. In increasing need of medical treatment, he resigned his commission as Governor of the Colony of New South Wales and, on 11th December 1792, sailed from Sydney on the *Atlantic*. We might imagine an emotional Phillip standing on the deck, watching the tiny settlement he had founded, which by now had become a small and growing township, receding into the distance as *Atlantic* drew further away from Sydney Cove. It may have been almost impossible for him not to have reflected on Sydney Cove in its virgin state almost five years earlier, before his party of convicts had hacked out the small clearing which would form the nucleus of the settlement, and he may have thought and perhaps even hoped that one day he might return.

Postscript to Arthur Phillip's Governorship

When Arthur Phillip stood on the deck of *Atlantic* and waved goodbye to Sydney Town, he was not alone. Bennelong and another young Wangal warrior, Yemmerrawanyea, had agreed to sail with him – Bennelong being particularly excited to see "The Land of The King". Their family and friends were greatly distressed, believing they would never see either of their kinsmen again.

After a six-month voyage from Sydney Cove, Bennelong and Yemmerrawanyea stepped into a totally alien world when the *Atlantic* docked at Falmouth, England on 19th May 1793. They were the first Indigenous Australians to visit England. From Falmouth, Phillip, Bennelong and Yemmerrawanyea proceeded by coach to London where Phillip had formal Georgian clothes tailored for the pair. In London, Bennelong and Yemmerrawanyea were accommodated at the home of William Waterhouse in Mayfair – Waterhouse being the father of Phillip's aide, Henry Waterhouse.

On 8th June 1793, Phillip took Bennelong and Yemmerrawanyea, resplendent in their newly tailored Georgian clothes, to the King's Theatre at the Haymarket to watch opera from a private box.[35] Some writers have suggested that the two Wangal men were presented to King George III. That may have occurred, yet there seems to be no documented evidence of such a meeting. They did visit St Paul's Cathedral and the Tower of London.

Despite Phillip's best efforts to present the two as diplomats or emissaries of the Eora people and notwithstanding the fine English clothes which they now wore, they were seen by the English as curiosities and exhibits of a strange and inferior race deemed incapable of governing themselves.

The English print media, showing entrenched views of British or white supremacy, were scathing of the two. A report carried in *Lloyd's Evening Post* London, was typical of sentiments expressed:

> *From the description given of the natives of Jackson's Bay they appear to be a race totally incapable of civilization, ... no inducement, and every means have been perseveringly tried, can draw them from a state of nature*[36]

Similar descriptions of Yemmerrawanyea and Bennelong continued in the London press. In September, *The Observer*, reported:

> *The two natives of New South Wales at present in this metropolis, are in appearance scarcely human; they continue to reside in Mount Street, Berkley square, in the neighbourhood of which they are to be seen daily; they cannot walk without the support of sticks, and appear to have lost all that agility they are said formerly to have possessed; one of them appears much emaciated; notwithstanding they are indulged in every inclination, they seem constantly dejected, and every effort to make them laugh has for many months past been ineffectual.*[37]

Clearly, by the time of this report, the two natives were suffering from depression and were longing for their homeland and their families. The one whom *The Observer* had referred to, above, as being "*much emaciated*" was the younger of the two, Yemmerrawanyea, who became increasingly ill in October 1793 with serious chest infections.

Bennelong and Yemmerrawanyea were then transferred to the home of Edward Kent in the village of Eltham, Kent, where they were cared for and attended to by Arthur Phillip and Mrs Phillip. Edward Kent was an employee of Lord Sydney, and Bennelong and Yemmerrawanyea met with Lord Sydney there. That could have given rise to some interesting discussion over dinner, for Lord Sydney was the one who had first pushed for the establishment of a British penal colony at Botany Bay – he was literally the father of the invasion.

After six months, Yemmerrawanyea seemingly recovered from his illness, though subsequent events showed that it had terminally weakened him.

On Wednesday 16th April 1794, Bennelong and Yemmerrawanyea were taken by Phillip to visit the Houses of Parliament at Westminster, causing uproarious protests in the House of Lords. *The Oracle & Public Advertiser*, reporting on their visit to Westminster, referred to them as *"the two sooty natives of New South Wales, brought over by Governor Phillip"*.[38]

Yemmerrawanyea died from a lung ailment on 18th May 1794 at the home of Edward Kent. He was nineteen years of age and was buried in St John's churchyard, Eltham. Phillip arranged for a granite headstone to be erected on his grave, bearing the inscription:

> *In Memory of Yemmerrawanyea,*
> *a Native of New South Wales,*
> *who died the 18th of May 1794*
> *In the 19th Year of his AGE.*

Bennelong finally returned to Sydney Cove on board *HMS Reliance* which departed England on 2nd March 1795 and docked in Sydney Cove on 7th September 1795. Accompanying Bennelong on that voyage was the much-awaited second Governor of the Colony of New South Wales, Captain John Hunter.

Arthur Phillip died in Bath, England, on 31st August 1814, having never returned to New South Wales.

Arthur Phillip's Legacy

Recently, I travelled along George Street, Sydney, all the way from the northern end of the street near The Rocks to Central Station. I walked from The Rocks and at Circular Quay found I was able board one of the modern trams that now run all the way to Central Station, indeed all the way to Randwick, if one desires.

Near the Queen Victoria Building, I left the tram and repaired to a nearby coffee shop where I could sit on the footpath and watch as Sydney passed by. As I sipped my coffee, I wondered what Arthur Phillip would have made of the place had he been able to accompany me on that journey along George Street. I am sure he walked along George Street many times, perhaps daily, though in his day it was little more than a shorter cobblestoned street. Surely, he could never have imagined that the street and city would develop into their modern day form. What would he have thought about the cafés, the coffee shops and the availability of food in such abundance? Would he have been proud, I wondered? He would certainly have been amazed at the displays of food available in the cafés, and I think he would have been very proud too, not only of George Street but of the huge, busy metropolis that has grown from the small fragmentary outpost of civilisation he established on the sandy shores of Sydney Cove more than two centuries earlier.

My coffee finished, I decided to walk the rest of the way to the southern end of George Street. As I approached Central Station, I was aware I was walking through the area that Phillip would have known as Brickfield Hill. In Phillip's day, it was an area serving the colony's growing need for bricks which were fired there and then transported down to the settlement for the construction of substantial buildings. It was also an area where a significant number of natives resided on the fringe of the settlement. Here, my thoughts turned to wondering how Phillip would have reacted, had we encountered, on our travels a large and noisy group of Indigenous Australians staging a protest march with the Aboriginal flag and with their banners and T-shirts emblazoned with their slogan, "Always Was, Always Will Be, Aboriginal Land!" What would Phillip have made of that? I suspect he probably would have thought, "Some things haven't changed all that much". I doubt he would have approached the group and apologised for his actions – for the British invasion of Aboriginal land. He would have believed he had done his duty to his King, though he may have been saddened by the obvious fact that, after almost two and a half centuries, we have not been able to resolve our differences and live as one nation. No, he would not have apologised, yet it seems to me that a national apology is very much needed as an important first step towards reconciliation.

Arthur Phillip was a man constrained by his times and by his duty to the King whom he served. He had been commissioned as a military officer to build a colony, not a prison but a colony, on foreign shores and to ensure its growth and success. He was in many ways a far-sighted Governor who saw that, to survive as a colony, New South Wales would need to progress to a civil administration. It would require, he knew, a system for emancipating the convicts and that alone was an intuitive leap of understanding for a man of his times.

He was caught in a difficult situation in which access to land was the pivotal issue – land essential for the survivability of the colony he had established, yet land that had always provided sustenance for the survivability of another race, the Aboriginal people. His orders, to establish a viable colony on Aboriginal land and to *"open an Intercourse with the Natives and to conciliate their affections"* were at odds with each other and conflict was inevitable.

It is important to note that the Aboriginal people were fighting not only for the land per-se, although the land was certainly important to them. The bigger issue was that, without access to their land, they were being driven to the point of starvation and extinction. They were fighting for their very survival. Given the "Hungry Years" that the colonists had experienced and how close they themselves had come to extinction through starvation, that was something Phillip

60

should have understood – he should have understood the importance of food resources to the Indigenous peoples in this harsh land. Perhaps he did understand – perhaps he knew that, by extending the white invasion of Aboriginal lands, he was risking the extinction of the Indigenous peoples. Perhaps he believed that to be the price that had to be paid for bringing the colony to a survivable state. He should certainly have made greater attempts to co-exist with the Indigenous peoples on what was, after all, their own land. Yet, to do so is always a low priority for the commander of any invading force – the survivability of one's own people always takes precedence over the interests of the vanquished.

The issue of access to land had established an irreconcilable difference between the Aboriginal view that they were people of the land, that they in fact *belonged* to the land, and the British view that the land was vacant and there for the taking. Within that difficult situation, with diametrically opposed objectives, Phillip had attempted to conciliate the Aboriginals as he had been instructed to do through his intercourse with Arabanoo and later with Bennelong. He would say he had done his duty to his King as ordered.

That is not to absolve Arthur Phillip of the claims against him – that he had driven Aboriginal people from their land, that he had armed ex-convicts and settlers to pursue that same end and that he had ordered the mass-murder and decapitation of Indigenous people. At times he seemed torn between personal desires to serve both the British Crown on the one hand and the Eora people on the other. Yet, as we have seen, when push came to shove, he did his duty to his King and advanced the cause of the Crown at the expense of the Indigenous peoples, ordering his military forces out in violent attacks against them.

The tracts of land that he opened up as new agricultural areas, by necessity, spread over a much greater area than Warrane to which the Eora were attempting to confine the settlement. Though he would have preferred peaceful relations with the Eora, Phillip knew that they would resist expansion of the colony. He knew the Aboriginal people were proud and brave people who would fight for their land and for their food resources. Yet, he also knew that, ultimately, guns would rule supreme over spears.

In Sydney's Royal Botanic Gardens, only a few city blocks from George Street where I had travelled with Phillip, stands a large, impressive monument known as the Governor Phillip Fountain, erected to memorialise the achievements of the nation's first Governor and his place in the nation's history. It is quite a beautiful fountain in a lovely setting, and Sydneysiders and visitors to the city can often be seen picnicking on the lawns around it. All of the picnickers, however, appear to be non-Indigenous Australians or foreign visitors. Indigenous Australians are rarely seen there.

An imposing statue of Phillip wearing a sword at his hip and holding a flag in his left hand stands atop the fountain on a high marble pedestal. In his right hand, he holds out a proclamation – the proclamation declaring New South Wales to be a colonial possession of the British King. The front side of the square pedestal carries his name and wording about the unveiling of the monument on 22nd June 1897 whilst the other three sides carry relief panels displaying images representing Justice, Education and Patriotism. Below that, the pedestal is flanked by large, bronze reclining figures of Neptune, Agriculture, Cyclops and Commerce. Lower still are four bronze ships' prows with pairs of large mythical fish, perhaps meant to be dolphins, spraying water into white marble basins. At the very bottom, indicative of their place in Australian society at the time, are small bas relief panels of Aboriginal people. It is difficult to escape the notion that the fountain infers late 19th century concepts of society and race. The imposing figure of Phillip stands in all magnificence at the top, while the Aboriginal people, shown only in small bas relief panels, are at the very bottom, below even the dolphins.

4

MILITARY RULE
1793 - 1795

When Arthur Phillip sailed away from Sydney Cove on 11th December 1792, he waved goodbye to a colony with a total British population of 4,221 souls, more than 3,000 of whom were convicts. He also left a colony without a governor. That is merely a statement of fact – it is not intended to be a criticism of Phillip leaving the colony without a governor, for he was ill and needed to return to England for medical treatment.

Throughout 1791-1792, however, Phillip had spent two years encouraging the spread of both public and private farms into the areas based around the government farm in Parramatta. The settlement at Parramatta was home to extensive government cornfields and a female factory where convict women worked producing convict clothing – slops – all protected by a garrison of the New South Wales Corps.

As Phillip had given land grants, mostly of 50 acre lots to emancipated ex-convicts, satellite settlements had sprung up in places around Parramatta – at Prospect to the south-west, Toongabbie to the west and The Ponds to the north-east. The Ponds would later be named The Field of Mars and was located along the present-day Kissing Point Road, Dundas. Inch by inch, mile by mile, European settlement had encroached upon the land of the Darug people, whose ancestral home extended from Parramatta to the fertile riverbanks of the Nepean-Hawkesbury river system at the foot of the Blue Mountains. The Darug called the river Deerubbin.

Stepping in to fill that void left by Phillip's departure was Major Francis Grose, Commander of the New South

Wales Corps. Grose promoted himself to the rank of Lieutenant-General and, in the absence of a governor, would rule as Lieutenant-Governor or Acting Governor, until such time as a new permanent governor would be appointed by the Colonial Office in London. Under Grose's administration, the colony changed considerably, and almost overnight. Whereas Phillip had been intent on establishing a colony under civil administration transitioning in an orderly and timely fashion towards a white, democratic society of free settlers and farmers, Grose was an unwavering military man who did not see the settlement as a colony but purely as a prison, albeit one without walls. A settlement established on a population of convicts and felons, he believed, had to be governed by tight military control.

Immediately, Grose abandoned Phillip's civil administration of the colony and handed all authority to the officers of the New South Wales Corps. He abolished the civil courts and gave all judicial authority over both military and civil matters to officers of the Corps, with magistrates under the authority of Captain Joseph Foveaux. Overnight, the role of the officers of the Corps changed totally. From what had been a security role in keeping the Indigenous people at bay and guarding both convicts and government facilities, the officers of the Corps now became functionaries of governance and the settlement moved to one directly under military rule.

In the very same week that Arthur Phillip departed the colony, Grose repealed Phillip's prohibition against the sale of alcohol to convicts, resulting in rapid and exponential growth of drunkenness and unruly behaviour, a situation which was exacerbated when Grose moved to permit officers of the Corps to use rum as payment for the labour of emancipated convicts and for purchasing goods and services. From its inception, the colony had very little coinage and rum had largely become the accepted currency. Grose allowed the officers of the Corps to gain a monopoly on the purchase of all imported rum and then to exchange it at rates of their own setting. Soon, under Grose's administration, the New South Wales Corps came to dominate the colony's economy – it would not be long before they earned their *nom de guerre of* "The Rum Corps".

In every way, Grose favoured the Corps officers over convicts and free settlers and when crops failed in 1793, he overturned Governor Phillip's policy of equal rations for all by cutting rations for convicts but not for members of the Corps. His predecessor, under instructions from England, had declined to issue land grants to serving members of the Corps but Grose, seemingly on his own initiative, issued grants of farming land to Corps officers, together with up to ten convict labourers provisioned at government expense. He encouraged the officers to become engaged in farming and trading activities and put in place regulations designed to give the officers of the Corps a trading monopoly. By the time he returned to England in 1794, the Corps officers held a firm dominance over all trade within the colony.

Meanwhile, sporadic Aboriginal resistance to the encroachment of farms and settlements on their land continued, especially in the areas west of Sydney Cove in Toongabbie, Prospect Hill and Parramatta though, in his reports to London, Grose makes little mention of it. He rarely writes about Indigenous resistance or about the killing of Aboriginals and, were it not for the writings of Deputy Judge Advocate David Collins, we might well have no record of such events.

In reading Grose's reports to London, it is difficult to escape the notion that he was at all times wanting to impress upon the authorities in the Colonial Office that it was military rule that would establish successful governance in New South

Wales. He often wrote in a self-aggrandizing manner, pointing out how he had improved things since the departure of his predecessor, Governor Phillip. On 29th April 1794, Grose wrote to The Right Hon. Henry Dundas, 1st Viscount Melville, trusted aide to British Prime Minister William Pitt and one of the most powerful politicians in Britain:

> *When Governor Phillip left this country the military officers were suffering in huts of the most miserable description. I have now the satisfaction to say they are all in good barracks. I am particular in stating what has been done since the departure of the Governor, not because I wish to arrogate any consequence or merit to myself, for very little is due to me; but because I wish to represent in the most favourable point of view the officers serving in the colony, to whose great exertions the promising appearance of it may be entirely attributed.*[39]

In the above extract Grose was clearly not only praising his own efforts, despite his protestation that *"very little is due to me"*, but was also applauding the officers of the Corps who, as has been noted, were a dishonest, exploitative and oppressive force who merited little commendation.

In the same letter, Grose informed Dundas that two farming settlements about five miles apart had been established on the banks of the Hawkesbury around Richmond Hill:

> *I have settled on the banks of the Hawkesbury twenty-two settlers, who seem very much pleased with their farms. They describe the soil as particularly rich, and they inform me whatever they have planted has grown in the greatest luxuriance.*[40]

Surveyor General Augustus Alt prepared a survey map showing the land allocations and the names of those holding the land, which Grose attached to his letter. Those two farming settlements had been established in January 1794 on the banks of the Hawkesbury River near Green Hills, later to be renamed Windsor, some 25 miles north-west of Parramatta.

The Hawkesbury was the ancestral home of the Darug people who were among the most hostile of the New South Wales natives. It was for that reason that Arthur Phillip, during his tenure as Governor, had not issued land grants on the Hawkesbury, believing it too far removed from the Sydney settlement for the provision of effective protection.

Spot-fires of Aboriginal resistance were now breaking out on the Cumberland Plain, south and west of the Sydney settlement, all the way to Parramatta and further afield to the satellite settlements, even to Mulgoa near present-day Penrith and into the fertile river areas of the Deerubbin. The rapid proliferation of farms and settlements, especially with the accompanying clearing of the land, gave rise to increased Aboriginal anger and resistance. As hunter-gatherers, the Indigenous people had, for millennia, used the bushland habitat for the gathering of edible vegetation and for the hunting of native animals like kangaroos. With the habitat reduced to cleared land with only tree stumps remaining, both of those food sources were denied to them. Some trees, also, were of totemic spiritual significance to the Darug people, to whom land ownership and personal use of the land were alien concepts. The European settlers, on the other hand, considered land given or sold to them by the colony's Governor to be their personal land to do with as they wished – land they would protect as their own by firing on Aboriginals seen on or crossing their land.

The farmers cleared their land and planted food crops, mostly maize (Indian corn) and, in the process, pulled up the wild yams, a primary food source on which the Aboriginal people depended. The yam beds, especially around creeks, ponds, and riverbanks disappeared, having been replaced with corn, thus reducing the Aboriginal people to a state of near starvation.

The natives could see no reason why the stealing of food should be the province of the white invaders alone. As the white settlers denied the Indigenous people their traditional food supplies, the Aboriginals retaliated by plundering the farmers' hard-won grain. Accustomed to collecting yams and other edible plants from the native bushland, the Aboriginals were left with little option but to steal corn from the farmers' fields. In consequence, violent confrontations increased across an ever-widening area.

By 1793, Pemulwuy was leading raids on settlers in districts beyond his own Bidjigal ancestral lands, venturing into Brickfield Hill (site of the present-day Sydney Central Railway Station) and west as far as Prospect and Toongabbie. His anger at the presence of European settlers on Aboriginal land was driving him to become bolder and more willing to take risks as he attempted to contain the Berewalgal to land they had already settled and, if possible, to drive them off that land.

For twelve years from 1794 onwards, a series of savage and bitter wars spread across the colony. The Frontier Wars ranged from the Cumberland Plain south and west of Botany Bay to Prospect and Parramatta and into the Hawkesbury from Richmond to Green Hills, then further down the Hawkesbury through Portland Head as far as Wiseman's Ferry. Frontier Wars, it should be noted, is plural. It was not one widespread offensive by Aboriginals to drive the invaders off their land. It was a series of uncoordinated attacks by different Aboriginal groups over a widespread area, each defending their ancestral lands from encroachment by the colonists. Yet, it would be an injustice to speak only in terms of attacks or skirmishes – it was a state of war. Settlers, soldiers, administrators and natives all spoke of it as such.

Breaking out like spot fires, Aboriginal warriors would raid a farm or a settlement, defend when counter-attacked by soldiers and settlers, then go quiet for a short time before striking again. Theirs was a guerrilla warfare tactic which left the Europeans not knowing where or when the Aboriginals would strike next.

Captain James Cook and botanist Joseph Banks had recorded in their journals that the natives of New Holland were a passive people who would retreat into the bush when challenged and should not be expected to put up an armed resistance. Lieutenant-General Grose, Acting Governor of the colony as he now was, the soldiers of the New South Wales Corps and the settler-farmers were discovering that Cook and Banks could not have been more wrong.

Travellers were not safe on the roads, often being attacked by groups of Aboriginal warriors and robbed of everything they had with them – including the clothes they wore. Escaped convicts, John Wilson and William Knight, had joined the Aboriginals and lived with them in the Hawkesbury.[41] Wilson was known to the Aboriginals as *Bunboe* and he, Knight and perhaps other escaped convicts now living with the Aboriginals taught them that a musket, once discharged, was useless until it could be reloaded, a process taking up to twenty seconds. Thus, the Aboriginals learned that a group of travellers with only one musket between them or a farmer on his land grant could be attacked with impunity once the musket had been discharged. Companies of soldiers, on the other hand, knew that they needed to fire their muskets in a staggered manner, one group reloading while the other group fired their muskets.

With raids and attacks happening almost daily on the frontiers of white settlement, individual incidents are far too numerous to list in their entirety, but a few examples will show the ferocity of the wars and the brutality of acts perpetrated on both sides.

At Toongabbie in April 1794, armed farmers guarding the fields of Indian corn (maize) shot three Aboriginal raiders and decapitated the bodies. To verify their story to authorities, they brought in one man's head in a bag. On 15th April 1794, Judge Advocate Richard Atkins wrote in his journal:

> *The head of one was brought in and the Lt. Govr.* [Francis Grose] *preserved it as a present for Dr. Hunter.*[42] (Words in brackets added by the author for clarification.)

In London, Surgeon John Hunter had died, so the head was sent on to Sir Joseph Banks who later provided the skulls of two "New Hollanders" to the German anatomist Johann Freidrich Blumenbach in Göttingen.[43]

In September of the same year, at the Hawkesbury settlement, Aboriginal warriors attacked and seriously injured a farmer and his convict labourer, stealing clothing and provisions. On this incident, Judge Advocate David Collins wrote:

> *At the Hawkesbury they* [the natives] *were not so friendly; a settler there and his servant were nearly murdered in their hut by some natives from the woods, who stole upon them with such secrecy as to wound and overpower them before they could procure assistance. A few days after this circumstance, a body of natives attacked the settlers, and carried off their clothes, provisions, and whatever else they could lay their hands on. The sufferers collected what arms they could, and, following them, seven or eight of the plunderers were killed upon the spot. This mode of treating them had become absolutely necessary, from the frequency and evil effects of their visits; but whatever the settlers at the river suffered was*

entirely brought on them by their own misconduct: there was not a doubt but that many natives had been wantonly fired upon, and when their children, after the flight of the parents, have fallen into the settlers hands, they have been detained at their huts, notwithstanding the earnest entreaties of the parents for their return.[44] (Words in brackets added by the author for clarification.)

The following month, October 1794, Hawkesbury settlers seized and killed a young Aboriginal boy whom they claimed was acting as a spy for Aboriginal raiders. Collins casts doubt on the settlers' version of events and suggests that they, in his words, *"merited the attacks"* made on them by Aboriginals:

Some accounts were received from the Hawkesbury, which corroborated the opinion that the settlers there merited the attacks which were from time to time made upon them by the natives; it being now said, that some of them had seized a native boy, and, after tying him hand and foot, had dragged him several times through a fire, until his back was dreadfully burnt, and in that state had thrown him into the river, where they shot and killed him. Such a report could not be heard without the closest examination; when it appeared, that a boy had actually been shot when in the water, from a conviction, as they said, of his being detached as a spy upon them from a large body of natives; and that he was returning to them with an account of their weakness; there being only one musket to be found among several farms. No person appearing to contradict this account, it was admitted as a truth; though many still considered it as a tale invented to cover the true circumstance, that a boy had been cruelly and wantonly murdered by them.[45]

Meanwhile, Pemulwuy was leading groups of warriors in raids against the British colonisers all over *Bidjigal* Country which extended along the Georges River from Botany Bay to Salt Pan Creek, near present-day Bankstown. Pemulwuy was the consummate guerrilla fighter, with inimitable knowledge of his own Country – knowledge bequeathed to him by his ancestors who had walked this land for thousands of years.

He and his *Bidjigal* warriors attacked isolated farms where they killed settlers and stole whatever was available – clothing, food, tools and weapons, including axes and hatchets – before burning the farmers' houses and their hard-won crops.

Part of the difficulty facing the colonisers in this ongoing war was the fact that, because they were establishing settlement outposts and farms, their assets were stationary and therefore vulnerable, whereas the Aboriginal raiders could move from place to place, reconnoitring targets and planning their attacks, with the colonists never knowing where or when they would next strike.

In December 1794, the Acting Governor, Lieutenant-General Grose, departed the colony and returned to England for medical treatment and recuperation. He was succeeded in the role of Lieutenant-Governor by his second in command of the New South Wales Corps, William Paterson ,who would administer the colony until the arrival of Governor John Hunter nine months later. It would be a tumultuous time.

The Battle of Richmond Hill on 7th June 1795 was the major conflict during the short-lived tenure of William Paterson. Four hundred settlers had moved into the Hawkesbury in the first six months of 1795, clearing land and planting Indian corn fields across a swath of land extending more than thirty miles on both sides of the Hawkesbury River.[39] Native yam beds, on which the Aboriginals depended as a primary food source, were ripped up and replaced with maize.

As the corn harvest time approached, settlers sent word to the Corps Commander at Parramatta, warning that

Aboriginal groups were gathering with intent to steal the corn harvest. In response, Paterson sent a company of sixty-eight soldiers of the Corps with instructions to join together with armed settlers to kill as many Aboriginals as they could find. To strike terror into any survivors, the soldiers were ordered to use gallows trees across the *Darug* Country and to hang thereon the bodies of all Aboriginals they might kill.[40]

Paterson was a ruthless military man and not one to deal in half-measures – his intent was to totally destroy or, failing that, to drive away the entire Aboriginal presence from the area of the Hawkesbury farms. The Battle of Richmond Hill, also known as the Massacre of Richmond Hill, took place between large numbers of *Darug* warriors and troops of the New South Wales Corps together with some armed settlers. The resulting massacre saw the killing of "seven or eight" Darug warriors, according to official reports,[48] though it is believed the actual number was considerably higher. In addition, at least ten were captured and taken to Sydney, including five women, one of whom was heavily pregnant and shot through the stomach, several children and a crippled, old man. The definitive number of Darug people who had died defending their rights to Country at Richmond Hill is not known.

Whilst constant attacks on unarmed settlers travelling lonely roads continued, together with sporadic maize raids on isolated farms across most parts of the colony, in the Hawkesbury, a state of open war existed between the settlers, supported by troopers, and the Darug. On 11th June 1795, Judge Advocate David Collins wrote to Edward Laing about the conflict:

> *The natives at the Hawkesbury are murdering the settlers – Abbott & MacKellar with Co soldiers are in turn, murdering the natives (but it cannot be avoided).*[49]

Acting Governor Patterson reported on 15th June 1795 that the Aboriginal hostility was so great that he may have to abandon the settlement on the Hawkesbury River altogether, despite having 60 soldiers permanently guarding the area.[50]

Yet, as the violence continued to escalate, Paterson was able to maintain and even increase the settlement on the Hawkesbury. On 7th September 1795, Governor John Hunter arrived at Sydney Cove on board *HMS Reliance* and assumed control of the troubled colony on 11th September 1795.

5

CONSOLIDATION
1795 – 1800

Governor John Hunter stepped off *HMS Reliance* and into a colony beset by increasing hostilities between the colonists and the Indigenous peoples. He had been issued the same generic instructions as had been given to his predecessor, Arthur Phillip – *to endeavour by every possible means to open an Intercourse with the Natives and to conciliate their affections, enjoining all Our Subjects to live in amity and kindness with them.*

The Hawkesbury settlement of Green Hills had become the third area of European settlement after Sydney and Parramatta, and such was the fertility of the riverbank soil along the Hawkesbury that it was becoming known as the granary of the colony. But, the fields of maize planted there by the settlers had replaced the wild yam fields on which the Darug people depended as a primary source of food. Payback Aboriginal raids on the maize crops and on the settlers' homes had increased, both in frequency and in ferocity, to the point that, in the words of David Collins, a state of *"open war"* existed between the settlers and the Darug from as early as April 1795, six months before the arrival of Governor Hunter.[51]

Fire was a weapon the Aboriginals used with devastating effect. They would raid the corn fields and the settlers' houses, carrying off everything they could, then set fire to the remnants of the corn fields, to the settlers' granaries and their houses. Settlers, comprising convicts who had served their time and been given land grants around South Creek and Green Hills, together with their convict labourers, united in reprisal attacks on the Indigenous people which only resulted in yet more payback attacks by the Aboriginals of the area. The district had quickly descended into a lawless frontier. Some soldiers of the New South Wales Corps were given small land grants at places around the Hawkesbury settlement as a means of providing security to settlers in the region.[43] It was largely an ineffective measure because the soldiers commonly drove the settlers into a heightened feeling of enmity with the Aboriginals and, in consequence, violence only increased.

The abduction of Aboriginal children by settlers in the Hawkesbury was relatively common practice during the years of the Frontier Wars. Aboriginal children, usually younger than ten years of age, were seized by settlers and soldiers who claimed that the children were orphans whose families had been killed in the inter-racial wars. Such was rarely the case and, when the families of abducted children came demanding the return of their children, they were more often than not driven away with further violence. Young children were chosen for abduction – young enough to be assimilated into white families, yet old enough to survive without parental care. As they grew older, these "rescued orphans" were forced to work as household servants and/or field labourers. Abducted female children were frequently used for the sexual gratification of their captors.

More than two centuries later, Prime Minister Kevin Rudd made a formal apology on behalf of the nation to the children and families of "The Stolen Generation". Rudd was *not* speaking of the children abducted during the Frontier Wars. He was apologising for the removal of children from their families by Australian federal and state government agencies, church missions and welfare agencies under acts of their respective parliaments during the period of approximately 1905 – 1970 when thousands of Aboriginal children were forcibly removed, to be raised in harsh institutions or adopted into non-Indigenous families. Notwithstanding the fact that those institutions may have believed they were acting in the best interests of the children, they were working within cruel and discriminatory policies which left thousands of Aboriginal families bereaved. Many parents would never see their children again and many of the children so taken would never know their birth parents. The national apology was long overdue.

Whilst Rudd's national apology did not address the children abducted during the Frontier Wars at the beginning of the nineteenth century, it is difficult to look back on those abductions and not conclude that those children, too, were part of a different stolen generation. Aboriginal women, too, were abducted and held as sex slaves, sometimes restrained in chains like wild animals. Many settlers and convicts referred to the practice of going in search of Indigenous women to be abducted as "gin hunting" and spoke of it in terms of a sporting contest. It was a deplorable term for a deplorable practice, and any modern-day white Australian who is not immeasurably shamed by the history of that practice and repulsed by the very mention of it, needs to engage in some serious introspection.

Yet, we should be careful not to judge all settlers and soldiers in the same manner. Some worked hard to establish an honourable and respectful rapport with the local Indigenous people. Some, recognising the importance of the native yam beds to the Aboriginals, left those parts of their land untouched and accessible to the Aboriginal people, notwithstanding the fact that the yam beds were usually the best part of the settler's land. Some tried hard to live in harmony, or at least in a live-and-let-live relationship with the Aboriginals. Invariably, their neighbours shook their heads and ridiculed them.

Despite the utter lawlessness of the Hawkesbury frontier, more and more settlers poured into the area and, by late 1796, were establishing small farms on both sides of the river all the way downstream to Portland Head, a huge U-shaped bend in the river which would later be named Sackville Reach. Some were given land grants, usually of fifty acres, but others simply squatted on a piece of ground, planted token crops to show they were engaged in cultivation and defied anyone to try and say it was not their land. Those around Portland Head were particularly vulnerable to Aboriginal attack because the riverbank floodplains, where they pulled up the yams and planted their maize crops, were very narrow with high, rocky ridges and heavily wooded hills behind them. Thus the settlers were hemmed in between the ridges on one side and the river on the other. Between 1794 and 1799, frequent Aboriginal raids occurred, especially approaching harvest time, which involved stealing corn and other supplies before burning crops and houses to the ground. Those raids forced some settlers to walk off their land which, of course, was the main objective of the Aboriginal warriors. Yet, for everyone who walked of his land, others came in a relentless stream, and Aboriginal raids, settler retaliation and Aboriginal payback continued unabated.

Meanwhile, on the Cumberland Plain, south and west of Sydney, the Bidjigal warrior Pemulwuy continued to lead a guerrilla war against isolated farms across his own Bidjigal Country. In March 1797, Pemulwuy led a raiding party of more than a hundred hostile warriors against the government farm at Toongabbie. It was, perhaps, the largest Aboriginal raiding force to that date and, to have amassed so many warriors, Pemulwuy must have enjoined warriors from outside his Bidjigal clan, drawing on the inter-clan marriage relationships to join in the attack. From his own clan, Pemulwuy would not have been able to amass more than twenty, or perhaps thirty, warriors. A large party of soldiers and armed settlers pursued the warriors to the outskirts of the Parramatta settlement, where the pursuit was called off, and the European forces repaired into the settlement to prepare for its defence, should Pemulwuy decide to attack.

They were given only one hour to prepare their defence before Pemulwuy led his warriors into the settlement where they confronted the soldiers and armed settlers. Pemulwuy, in a rage, threatened to spear the first man who approached him and did so when a soldier stepped forward. In the next few moments, which would be recorded as "The Battle of Parramatta", the warriors launched their spears and the defenders opened fire with their muskets. Muskets, of course, won the day and many Aboriginal warriors were immediately killed. It was later claimed that half the Aboriginal warriors – around fifty – were killed or seriously wounded by musket shot.[51] Pemulwuy himself was felled and severely wounded, having been shot several times with buckshot to the head and legs. He was chained and taken alive to the Parramatta hospital where he was held in leg irons. For several days, he was in and out of consciousness and the government doctors believed he would soon expire from his wounds. Yet, somehow, against all odds, he recovered and escaped from the hospital, still in his leg irons. A few weeks later, he was sighted in his Bidjigal Country near Botany Bay. His escape from the Parramatta hospital gave rise to the widely held belief amongst the Eora people that Pemulwuy was a clever man or a doctor, a *carradhy* in their language, who could heal wounds. Thus, the Pemulwuy legend grew – that he could not be killed by firearms. Governor Hunter stated his firm conviction that, ultimately, this belief would be proven wrong:

> *A strange idea was found to prevail among the natives respecting the savage Pe-mul-wy, which was very likely to prove fatal to him in the end. Both he and they entertained an opinion, that, from his having been frequently wounded, he could not be killed by our*

⟷ ∞ ⟷

On 6th July 1797, Governor John Hunter wrote to the Duke of Portland, reporting survivors of a merchant vessel which had been wrecked on a voyage from Calcutta to Sydney some five months earlier, in February 1797. The ship, originally named the *Begum Shaw*, was a 300 ton sailing vessel which normally operated between Calcutta and the Persian Gulf. In 1796, the ship had been sold to the Anglo-Indian trading company of Campbell & Clarke, renamed the *Sydney Cove*, and prepared for merchant voyages carrying speculative cargo, including large shipments of rum, from Calcutta to the penal colony in Port Jackson. The vessel was probably ill-suited for voyages across the Southern Ocean.

The *Sydney Cove* sailed from Calcutta on 10th November 1796 with a crew of fifty, including Captain Guy Hamilton, five other European crewmen and forty-four Bengali sailors – Lascars. The *Sydney Cove* sprang a leak in the Southern Ocean and was lucky to reach as far as she did, finally being beached on a small island north-east of Van Diemen's land. All on board made it safely to shore where they set up camp. Realising they had little hope of rescue from the remote island unless they could, by their own efforts, reach the settlement at Port Jackson, seventeen men – four European crewmen and thirteen Lascars - set out in the ship's longboat, crossing the treacherous waters of what would later be known as Bass Strait, headed for Port Jackson and Sydney Cove, more than four hundred nautical miles north. At a point now known as Ninety Mile Beach in Gippsland, Southeast Victoria, the longboat, too, was wrecked, leaving the party of seventeen with no option other than to attempt a walk of almost 400 miles to Port Jackson. Only three of them would make it, barely alive.

In his report to the Duke of Portland, Governor Hunter would write:

In May last, a small rowboat, fishing to the southward of Botany Bay, discovered three people on the shore, whom they took into the boat and brought hither scarcely alive. The remainder of the seventeen have undoubtedly perished or been killed by the natives, these survivors having been much annoyed and wounded by them. On their arrival they gave an account of two others whom they had left a small distance from the place where they met the boat, but too weak to proceed further. Upon this information I immediately sent a whaleboat well manned and put on board everything which could be necessary for people in that condition, as well as cloathing [sic] as [sic] nourishing articles of food and sent the same fishermen who had taken up the others in this boat, but these unfortunate men were not to be found. Some articles they had were picked up covered with blood, so that we have reason to believe they have been murdered in this helpless state.[53]

Those who had been left on the island where the *Sydney Cove* had been beached, Captain Guy Hamilton and thirty-two Lascars, were later rescued by ships dispatched from Port Jackson and the island was thenceforth known as Preservation Island. But, of the seventeen who had set out in the longboat, fourteen had almost certainly been killed by natives – by the Yuin people whose Country was the south coast of New South Wales. The incident, however, would soon lead to interest in another natural resource and extend colonial exploration into other parts of Aboriginal land.

Meanwhile, in February 1798, with the maize crops ripening, Pemulwuy stuck again, his warriors killing a settler and wounding three others at Toongabbie. Days later, they struck again, killing two more settlers in the same district. Governor Hunter, seemingly with some reluctance, was forced to respond by again sending troops to Toongabbie to subjugate the natives. With reference to this incident, Judge Advocate David Collins wrote:

> *It became, from these circumstances, absolutely necessary to send out numerous well-armed parties, and attack them* [the natives] *wherever they should be met with; for lenity or forbearance had only been followed by repeated acts of cruelty.*[54] (Words in brackets added by the author for clarification.)

As the Frontier Wars continued on the Cumberland Plain and in the Hawkesbury, Hunter was frequently required to dispatch military forces to protect the lives of settlers – settlers who might not have merited such protection. In his dealings with the Indigenous people, Hunter seems to have been more restrained, both in comparison with his predecessors and with those who would follow. He seemingly agreed with Judge Advocate David Collins, who had left the colony in August 1796, that the settlers *"merited the attacks which were from time to time made upon them by the natives,"*[55] and that such attacks had often been brought upon the settlers *"by their own misconduct."*[56]

Indeed, Hunter's opinion of the settlers' morality could not have been more scathing, and he would write to the Duke of Portland, stating:

> *A more wicked, abandoned and irreligious set of people have never been brought together in any part of the world. My support of the clergy and the countenance which they are entitled to, and which, as a most necessary and essential part of that civil police they will always receive from me, has not been much relished by the colony at large, because order and morality is not the wish of*

its inhabitants; it interferes with the private views and pursuits of individuals of various descriptions.[57]

He was no more enamoured with the men and officers of the New South Wales Corps and wrote to Portland on that issue also:

I should feel myself deficient in that duty which I owe to his Majesty's service in this part of the world were I not to take a liberty which I have no reason to believe your Grace will be offended at — I mean, in remarking that the manner in which this corps has, since employed upon this service, been recruited does in a great measure weaken the effect or service which we would expect to derive from the assistance of the military. Soldiers from the Savoy,[58] and other characters who have been considered as disgraceful to every other regiment in his Majesty's service have been thought fit and proper recruits for the New South Wales Corps, which, in my humble opinion, my Lord, should have been composed of the very best and most orderly dispositions.[59]

In September 1799, settlers in Green Hills tortured and murdered two Aboriginal boys who, together with one other, had brought to the farm the musket of Thomas Hodgkinson, a settler who had recently been killed in the bush by natives. The three boys were well known to the settlers and were frequent visitors to the farm. Yet, because they were carrying Hodgkinson's musket, they were attacked and tortured by the settlers. One, Little Jemmy, was shot and one, Little George, hacked to pieces by swords. The third boy, Little Charley, escaped by diving into the river. Later, a Hawkesbury Aboriginal elder, Yellowgowey, would claim that Hodgkinson had been killed by a notorious Aboriginal warrior named Major White.[60] The three Aboriginal boys, it seems, had been merely returning Hodgkinson's musket to the farm.

Governor Hunter had the murderers arrested and brought to trial where they were found guilty of the murders but then released on the grounds that their farms were now in danger of being destroyed by payback attacks from the natives.

> *Those men found guilty of murder,* Governor Hunter wrote to the Duke of Portland, *are now at large and living upon their farms, as much at their ease as ever. I conceive, from the nature of the Governor's authority, I might have rejected the bail and kept the prisoners under confinement until the effect of the special reference was known; but I have been unwilling to shew the colony that any difference is likely to take place between the judicial and executive authoritys* [sic], *particularly when in the smallest degree inconsistent with lenity.*[61]

The Governor was also at pains to point out to Portland that the number of natives being killed was disproportionately large when compared to the number of white settlers killed:

> *You will discover, my Lord, what a host of evidence is brought forward from that quarter to prove what numbers of white people have been killed by the natives; but could we have brought with equal ease such proofs from the natives as they are capable of affording the wanton and barbarous manner in which many of them have been destroyed, and to have confronted them with those of the white inhabitants, we should have found an astonishing difference in the numbers.*[62]

Hunter, furthermore, appears to have been the first administrator of the colony to understand that the natives were to be considered as British subjects (whether they wanted to be so considered or not) and, as such, were deserving of British rights and protections. In his report to Portland about the killing of the two young aboriginals, and about the trial of the killers, Hunter referred to his original instructions, to *"open an intercourse with the natives and to conciliate their affections"*. Hunter declared to Portland that:

> *Every information within my power respecting the light in which
> the natives of this country were to be held as a people now under
> the protection of His Majesty's Government was laid before the
> court.*[63]

A full transcript of the trial proceedings relating to this incident was attached to Hunter's letter to the Duke of Portland.[64]

Yet, powerful forces within the colony were working against the Governor. Almost from the day of his arrival, Hunter had been engaged in an incessant struggle to overcome and regulate the abuses of the Rum Corps which had been encouraged and allowed to develop under the administrations of Grose and Paterson. His pleas for support from the Duke of Portland in England went largely ignored, in the main because powerful entities within New South Wales were undermining Hunter's authority through letters privately sent to Portland. In fairness, the British government at the time was likely preoccupied with bitter wars against the French, and with the Irish rebellion of 1798 – by comparison with such lofty affairs of state, the pleas of the Governor of a small penal colony on the other side of the world were of little importance.

As early as mid-1797, Hunter was aware of anonymous and slanderous documents being disseminated within the colony, besmirching his name and character and alleging his involvement in the very practices he was endeavouring to eradicate. On 1st June 1797, he wrote about the matter to the Duke of Portland:

> *An anonymous paper having lately been dropt* [sic] *in the streets,
> in which its author is endeavouring to lug my name into that
> vortex of dirty traffic which I have been labouring to put a stop
> to; this you will perceive by a Public Notice and reward I have
> offered for the discovery of the author or adviser (21st June) but I*

have not succeeded. The reward is such that had it been wholly amongst the lower classes it would have had effect. I feel myself so invulnerable from such attacks that, altho' they make me angry, I most heartily despise them, but will not fail to search for its author as long as I remain here.[65]

The Duke of Portland, one of three Secretaries of State within the British government, was already aware of the accusations against the Governor. He had received letters from officers of the New South Wales Corps, including from John Macarthur, charging Governor Hunter with participation in the very abuses he had been striving so hard to eliminate and in which they, the very writers of those letters, were themselves complicit. Typical of the manner in which Macarthur and others were undermining the authority and office of the Governor were accusations of maladministration of the colony. Macarthur wrote to Portland:

… and I hesitate not to say further, that the interest of Government [meaning the British home government] *is utterly disregarded, its money idly and wantonly squandered, whilst vice and profligacy are openly countenanced.*[66] (Words in brackets added by the author for clarification.)

In response to those letters, Portland then called upon Governor Hunter to respond to the accusations against him and his officers, without informing the Governor of the names of his accusers. Hunter's bitterness, anger and disgust were not hidden with the words of his response to Portland:

It is not in my power, my Lord, to furnish language sufficiently expressive of my extreme astonishment and sincere regret at the contents of your Grace's separate letter…

Let those even whose conduct have compelled me, as a duty I owe to His Majesty's service, to complain to your Grace appear openly and fairly, and attempt to show in the most trifling degree any one act of mine at which I ought to blush, and they will find me prepared to meet them.[67]

The power and influence of the Rum Corps had reached all the way to London and, in April 1800, Hunter received a dispatch from the Duke of Portland, dated 5th November 1799, recalling him to England. Notification of his recall was carried by his successor, Philip Gidley King, who arrived on the store ship *Speedy* on 20th April 1800, with orders to assume the office as Governor as soon as Hunter was able to depart. King, already frustrated by delays in his departure from England, and despite his former friendly association with Hunter, was eager to assume office, and the final months of Hunter's governorship were impacted by acrimony between his successor and him. King's unseemly desire to be rid of Hunter as soon as possible led to a bitterness between the two, reflected in their frequent writings one to the other. On 8th July 1800, Governor Hunter wrote to King, his Lieutenant-Governor, expressing his resentment at King's indecorous impatience for him to be gone:

> *I received your letter of the 6th, which I cannot but feel as an aggravation of those indirect insults which I have experienced since your arrival; and I must say that they have been such as I do not feel myself disposed, either as a publick officer or a private person, to submit to. That indelicate impatience so conspicuously manifested in you for being the possessor of my office, and which I confess myself no less impatient to put into yours or any other hands, until I can have the opportunity to convince His Majesty's Minister as well of the imposition practised upon his well-known justice as of the injury done to me. Your impatience, I say, and the various threatnings you have so publickly held out of what your intentions were, have occasioned suggestions among the people in several parts of this country, not only effecting my authority and respectability as the Governor, but injurious to my character as*

an officer and a man. It has been believed, sir, from these causes, and the observations which have been made, that you possessed a power to annul my authority altogether, and to render me, who have so long commanded here with justice, humanity, honour, and integrity, a mere cypher.[68]

Hunter finally handed over the governorship to King on 28th September 1800 and sailed for England on board *Buffalo*, arriving at Spithead on 24th May 1801.

Anxious to vindicate himself and his reputation, he sought a public inquiry into the charges made against him and his administration, seeking to bring into the realm of public knowledge the identities of those who had undermined him as Governor. His request for an inquiry was denied and the Duke of Portland ignored numerous requests by Hunter for an audience.

Governor John Hunter appears to have been a man loyal to his post as His Majesty's representative in New South Wales, desiring only to improve the state of the colony even whilst being under constant subversive attack from others with vested self-interests within the colony. His administration may have lacked some of the drive and energy of his successor, some twenty years his junior, yet he should be respected for the even-handed approach which he endeavoured to implement in his dealings with the Indigenous peoples of New South Wales. It is true that he did, on occasions, send out regiments of the New South Wales Corps to quell Indigenous unrest, but when reading from his dispatches it seems he did so reluctantly and with a heavy heart. He appears to have been a man desirous of harmonious relations with the Indigenous peoples – harmonious relations which, in the main, had been rendered all but impossible by the ruinous actions of the settlers themselves. Furthermore, as we have seen, he appeared to be the first administrator of the colony who recognised that, under British law, Indigenous people of the colony were British subjects and entitled to the protection of British law.[69]

Had he received the support he merited from the Duke of Portland, it is likely that Hunter's administration would have initiated much needed reforms and led to a more harmonious and prosperous colony. His recall to England was undeserved, and the failures of his administration should, in large measure, be placed at the feet of the Duke of Portland and subversive officers within the colony.

6
TERRITORIAL EXPANSION
1800 – 1806

Philip Gidley King assumed office as Governor of the Colony of New South Wales on 28th September 1800 and began by issuing a number of General Orders which he had been busy preparing whilst waiting for his predecessor to move on. His abiding intent was to reform the economy of the colony by curbing the exploitative monopoly that officers of the New South Wales Corps held over most items of trade, especially, but not exclusively, in the trade of rum. He would have some successes in his attempts to restructure the economy and to ease the burden on the small, poorer settlers but he was fought all the way by the Rum Corps and he was unable to entirely suppress their influence and excesses. He established breweries, thus offering the settlers a cheaper and more accessible alternative to rum and, over the course of his governorship, managed to reduce the amount of imported rum by about thirty percent. Yet, in the process he had to deal increasingly with domestic illegal distilling of rum within the colony. He established a government store, importing merchandise from Britain and other places and sold it at prices which further weakened the Corps' monopolistic grip on the economy. Yet the government store was beset with difficulties because supplies were irregular and unreliable.

By the time Governor King took office, the areas of white settlement were rapidly expanding across the Cumberland Plain south and west of Sydney and along the Hawkesbury. Governor Arthur Phillip's original instructions from the Colonial Office were that free settlers and emancipated convicts who were *"of good conduct and disposition to industry"* could receive land grants on the basis of thirty acres to an individual male, an additional twenty acres if married, and an additional ten acres for each child with him at the time of the grant.[70] Officers and men of the marines were not entitled to land grants under these orders but, in August 1789, Phillip had received additional orders entitling non-commissioned officers of the marines to one hundred acres and privates to fifty acres, over and above such acreage as would be granted to them if they had been emancipated convicts.[71] Under these new orders, commissioned officers remained notably ineligible for land grants for they were expected to concentrate on their military duties rather than on farming and commercial pursuits. Phillip had been given sole discretion over the allocation of land grants and gave grants only to those he thought most likely to succeed and make a positive contribution to the development of the young colony. By the time of his departure from the colony in December 1792, he had awarded only 4,000 acres in land grants.

It was Acting Governor Francis Grose, during the period of military rule following the departure of Arthur Phillip, who commenced making large scale land grants to his fellow commissioned officers of the Corps in 1792. Grose favoured the officers of the Corps, especially his friends and cronies, in many ways, thus giving them the means to exploit the settlers and small landholders through their iron-like grip on the economy. Yet, it was the granting of land to officers of the Corps which most impacted the Indigenous peoples by forcing them further and further away from white settlement areas. In 1793, Grose had granted his crony, John Macarthur, one hundred acres at Rose Hill, of some of the best land that had been discovered, with unrestricted access to convict labour. Later that same year Macarthur was granted a further one hundred acres which made him one of the largest landholders in the colony with two hundred acres of good land on which he established the "Elizabeth Macarthur Farm", named in honour of his wife. During the latter half of the last decade of the eighteenth century, Grose, his successor Lieutenant-Governor William Paterson and, from 1795 onwards, Governor Philip Gidley King, made greater and greater land grants to officers of the Corps – notwithstanding the fact that many of these were not used for agricultural purposes but as collateral for exploitation and land speculation.

The expansion of farming and pastoral holdings outpaced even the government allocation of land grants as squatters with no legal claim to land established farms and sheep runs in new territories. Those squatters who concentrated on establishing sheep runs, as opposed to those who established agricultural farms, earned for themselves the somewhat honorific title of 'the squattocracy'. The spread of small agricultural farms and pastoral runs, of course, all resulted in further dispossession of Aboriginal peoples from their lands, and ongoing conflict over land and access to food resources was inevitable.

By 1801, tensions between John Macarthur and Governor King were intensifying, as indeed they had between Macarthur and the previous Governor, John Hunter. Macarthur excluded the Governor from his social circle and convinced most of the officers of the Corps to do likewise. The Commanding Officer of the Corps, Lieutenant-Colonel William Paterson, however, refused to do so because of the close association between his wife and the Governor's wife. When Macarthur attempted to bend Paterson to his will by threatening to reveal private, salacious details concerning Paterson's wife, Paterson challenged Macarthur to a duel.

The duel, on 14th September 1801, resulted in Macarthur severely wounding Paterson, his superior officer. Governor King reacted by having Macarthur charged with dissent, a charge approaching that of mutiny and, when

Macarthur requested that he be brought before a court-martial to clear his name, the Governor saw it as an opportunity to rid himself of his nemesis, at least temporarily. Recognising Macarthur's influence over almost all officers of the Corps, Governor King declared that any such court-martial in New South Wales would be but a sham in which Macarthur would be acquitted of all charges. Thus, he ordered Macarthur dispatched on the next ship to England. Macarthur would have his court martial, the Governor believed, but it would be in England, without the protection of his cronies.

The ship carrying Macarthur to England also carried a long, unflattering description of Macarthur's person in which Governor King did his very best to convey the contempt in which Macarthur was held by many within the Colony of NSW. He wrote:

> *Experience has convinced every man in this colony that there are no resources which art, cunning, impudence and a pair of basilisk eyes can afford that he does not put in practice to obtain any point he undertakes.*[72]

In England, however, Macarthur was not court-martialled. The Military Advocate-General recognised that he was dealing with a political hot-potato and determined that, as the offence had been committed in New South Wales, Macarthur should be returned to his regiment and court martialled there. Macarthur thereupon immediately resigned his commission as officer of the Corps and set about ingratiating himself to important and influential persons, none more so than the Colonial Secretary, Lord Camden.

Before Macarthur had left New South Wales, the British government was already assessing sheep fleeces that had been sent to Sir Joseph Banks by Governor King. Britain, engaged in the Napoleonic war with France and Spain, was in need of supplies of wool, primarily but not exclusively for its military uniforms. Propitiously, Macarthur had taken with him to England specimens of fleeces from his own flock.

By virtue of his devious cunning, artful craftiness and some advantageous circumstances and driven by his conviction that the Napoleonic war would push wool prices high, Macarthur presented himself to the British government as one having a monopoly of authority within the New South Wales wool industry.

Say what we will of John Macarthur, and most of it is unflattering, he was a man capable of bending others to his will. He left England, bound for Sydney on the whaler *Argo*, secure in the knowledge that he had approval from the Colonial Office for the development of the New South Wales wool industry under his personal supervision. Furthermore, during the voyage, he was able to procure part-ownership of the *Argo* and to switch its purpose to a merchant ship under his management

On arrival at Sydney on 8th June 1805, Macarthur presented Governor Philip Gidley King with a written dispatch from the Colonial Secretary, Lord Camden, ordering Governor King to provide Macarthur a grant of five thousand acres of the best pastureland in the district known as Cowpastures. The order went on to state that a further five thousand acres would be granted if evident and tangible results were forthcoming from Macarthur's intended wool production scheme. Camden had promised Macarthur that the five thousand acres would be granted at a location of Macarthur's choosing and Macarthur had subsequently informed Camden that he wished to establish his wool production scheme at Cowpastures.

Governor King was reluctant to grant five thousand acres to Macarthur but was obliged to defer to Camden's orders. Cowpastures, however, was a district on the

Cumberland Plain, so named because a herd of cattle, escaped from Sydney, had been found happily grazing and reproducing in large number on the pastures there. Governor King initially refused to grant Macarthur his acreage at Cowpastures, and wrote about it to Edward Cooke, Under-Secretary of State:

> *By Mr. Macarthur who arrived here on 6th June, I had the honour of receiving My Lord Camden's and your Letters, dated October 30th, 1804; every arrangement respecting Mr. Macarthur and the object of his pursuit has and will be complied with except that of locating Ground about Mount Taurus on Cowpastures plains, which His Lordship might not have known or considered at the time is the resort of numerous herds of wild cattle. I have therefore left that Instruction until His Lordship's further pleasure is received thereon.*[73]

Yet, Macarthur's influence over Lord Camden prevailed and, ultimately, Governor King was forced to grant him the land at Cowpastures. Macarthur named his run "Camden Park" in honour of his benefactor. Today, the general area is known as Camden. It was the first area to be granted on the west bank of the Nepean River and, of course, it drove Indigenous people further from the riverbanks, where they procured a staple food source – yams.

Further exploration of the colony, which in the early colonial period included present-day New South Wales, Queensland, Victoria, South Australia, The Northern Territory and Tasmania, as well as Norfolk Island, would open up other areas of Aboriginal land for dispossession by settlers and by the Crown as the colonial government sought to exploit further resources of the land. By virtue of that exploration another burgeoning industry was about to push Aboriginal people even further off their land – the discovery of the colony's first export commodity, coal.

In 1796, William Clarke and other survivors of the wrecked ship *Sydney Cove* [74] had noticed coal exposed in the cliff south of Botany Bay. Two of their party had died there, but Clarke and the remaining two survivors made a fire to attract the attention of rescuers fishing offshore in a small boat. Rescued by the fishermen, the three survivors took with them lumps of coal that William Clarke showed to Governor John Hunter who immediately dispatched George Bass to find and report on the deposit. Bass found the coal at a place later to be named Coalcliff but reported that there were no safe harbours to facilitate the loading of coal.[75]

In September 1797, however, Lieutenant John Shortland, RN, had discovered a significant layer of good quality coal near the mouth of a river north of Sydney which he named the Hunter River, in honour of Governor John Hunter. When Philip Gidley King assumed office in September 1800, perhaps because of ongoing animosity with his predecessor, he continued for some time referencing the river in his dispatches as Coal River. The small island near the mouth of the river, later to be named Nobby's Head, he referred to as Coal Island.

Coal mining developed faster in the northern coalfields around Coal River than in the Coalcliff district south of Botany Bay because of the better harbour facilities found there, notwithstanding the fact that the entrance to the river around Coal Island, was narrow and treacherous. Nonetheless, the discovery and mining of coal around the Hunter/Coal River played an important part in the expansion of the colony beyond the Sydney, Parramatta and Hawkesbury settlements. On 19th June 1801, Governor King dispatched a party of soldiers and convicts in *HMS Lady Nelson*, commanded by Lieutenant James Grant, to establish a penal settlement at the mouth of the Hunter River, the site now known as the city of

Newcastle. There, convicts were employed both in mining coal and harvesting trees for timber. The tree fellers, in particular, were often brutal in their engagements with the local Aboriginal people, and sporadic violent engagements between the two ensued, probably because the Aboriginals were incensed about the felling of trees in their Country.

On 3rd July 1801, King wrote to the Duke of Portland informing him that all coal and timber being sourced from the Hunter River district had been declared "Crown Property":

> *The Governor judging it necessary for the public interest to declare the coals and timber which are to be procured at Hunter's River, to be the exclusive property of the Crown, and having thought fit to establish a port at Freshwater Bay, within that view, he strictly forbids any boat or vessel going there for coal, timber, or any other purpose, without obtaining a special license from the Governor's Secretary, stating the purpose of such voyage.*[76]

Ongoing exploration beyond Newcastle in the north and Coalcliff in the south, however, was extending colonial intrusion into Aboriginal habitats in yet other parts of the area then known as New South Wales. As early as 1797, George Bass had sailed a whaleboat along the unexplored coast south of Botany Bay, reaching into the stretch of rough ocean which would later be named Bass Strait. Because of the rough water, Bass was unable to proceed beyond a large bay which he named Western Port Bay, so named because it was the most western harbour yet discovered. Ironically, had Bass been able to proceed a little further westward, he would have found the much larger harbour, later to be named Port Phillip – now site of the city of Melbourne. Thus, Western Port became something of a misnomer because it actually lies east of Port Phillip. At Western Port, Bass encountered the Bunurong Aboriginal nation who lived there, existing mainly on shellfish,

100

kangaroos, possums and mutton birds. The Bunurong were not welcoming and, perhaps partly because of that, Bass returned to Sydney and recommended to the then Governor, John Hunter, that Western Port was unsuitable for white settlement. From the early years of the nineteenth-century however, Western Port was frequented by Sydney based seal hunters who faced periodic attacks from the Bunurong people.

With the exception of Sydney, where the Indigenous people were gradually becoming urbanised, the Frontier Wars between white and black continued across all parts of the colony where the white settlers and soldiers went. Payback, and payback for payback, made it difficult at times to determine whether it was the whites or the blacks who were responsible for initiating the violence. Yet, it must be said that, even when it was the Aboriginals who were the aggressors, it was they who held the moral high ground because they were resisting the invasion of their own Country and were, in most cases, being driven to the point of starvation by being refused access to their staple food sources.

Raiding parties of Aboriginal warriors continued across the Cumberland Plain and, on 1st May 1801, Governor King issued a Government and General Order authorising soldiers to fire upon natives in the Parramatta, George's River and Prospect Hill districts.

From the wanton manner in which a large body of natives, resident about Parramatta, George's River, and Prospect Hill, have attacked and killed some of Government sheep, and their violent threat of murdering all the white men they meet, which they put into execution by murdering Daniel Conroy, stockkeeper, in a most savage and inhumane manner, and severely wounding Smith, settler; and as it is impossible to foresee to what extent their present hostile menaces may be carried out, both with respect to the defenceless settlers and the stock, the

Governor has directed that this as well as all other bodies of natives in the above district to be driven back from the settlers' habitations by firing at them. But this order does not extend to the natives in any other district; nor is any native to be molested in any part of the harbour, at Sydney, or on the road leading to Parramatta.[77]

It was a somewhat restrained order, limiting as it did firing upon the troublesome natives to a restricted area and was, perhaps, indicative of King's desire to live peaceably with any natives who were prepared to live in accord with, and in submission to, white rule, as did the native population of Sydney. Yet, even in respect to the native attacks around Parramatta, occasioning the issuing of King's order, there remained those who were of the opinion that it was the whites who had precipitated the violence. George Caley, a naturalist, explorer and employee of Sir Joseph Banks, wrote to Banks stating that he had every reason to believe that the whites had been the *"greatest aggressors on the whole"*.[78]

In the twenty-first century, when we see one nation aggressively invading another, the defending soldiers are feted as patriots and heroes, worthy of our support. They are the ones holding the moral high ground. A case in point would be the 2022 invasion of the Ukraine by Russia. There is no reason we should not view the Indigenous peoples of Australia in the same way, as patriots defending their ancestral lands – except, of course, that their story cuts a little closer to the bone and shames those of us who are white Australians.

One native who was undoubtedly seen as an ongoing aggressor by the colonists, though arguably with good cause, was the Bidjigal warrior Pemulwuy whom Governor King held to be responsible for orchestrating the attacks around Parramatta and George's River. Folklore persisted that Pemulwuy could not be killed by firearms, and King was determined to prove that wrong.

102

Two outlawed escaped convicts, William Knight and Thomas Thrush, were believed to have been living with the natives and engaging with them in "*the most diabolical and outrageous offences on the public*"[79] which prompted Governor King, on 17th November 1801, to issue rewards of spirits, emancipation, free pardons and the granting of free convict labour, depending upon the circumstances of any person who could apprehend them.

Less than one week later, on 22nd November 1801, King issued a General Order extending that reward to include the Bidjigal warrior Pemulwuy:

> *It being known that William Knight and Thomas Thrush (outlaws) and the native, Pemulwuy, are the promoters of the outrageous acts that have been lately committed by the natives, whereby two men have been killed, several dangerously wounded, and numbers robbed, the reward advertised on the 17th instant will be given to those who will bring the above delinquents in, dead or alive.*[80]

On 1st March 1802, King wrote to the Duke of Portland advising him of the General Order above and of the rewards that had been offered to any person who could bring in Pemulwuy, Knight and Thrush, dead or alive.[81]

On 2nd June 1802, after twelve years of resistance, Pemulwuy's luck finally ran out when, along with another native, he was shot and killed. Some records indicate that he was shot by one Henry Hacking, sailor on the RN ship *Lady Nelson*, but that claim is difficult to verify and King, in his dispatches, refers to the killer(s) only as "*two settlers*".[82]

King's letter to Lord Hobart of 30th October 1802, reporting on the incident, is more than a little ambiguous. The

Governor appears to be stating that Pemulwuy was shot by white settlers, but that it was other Aboriginals, wanting to ingratiate themselves to the Governor, who brought in the severed head:

> *I gave orders for every person doing their utmost to bring Pemulwuy in either dead or alive, and as it is a practice strictly observed among the natives that murder should be atoned by the life of the murderer or someone belonging to him, the natives were told "that when Pemulwuy was given up they should be readmitted to our friendship." Sometime after two settlers, not having means of securing the persons of Pemulwuy and another native, shot them. On this event they* requested that Pemulwuy's head might be carried to the Governor and that as he (Pemulwuy) was the cause of all that had happened, and all anger being dropped on their part, they hoped I would allow them** to return to Parramatta. Orders were immediately given to that effect and not to molest or ill-treat any native.*[83]

Notes:
* * Does "they" refer to the settlers who shot Pemulwuy or to the natives?
* **Presumably in this instance "them" refers to the natives

Pemulwuy's head was preserved in spirits[84] and was then sent to Sir Joseph Banks in England, together with a letter in which King wrote:

> *Although a terrible pest to the colony, he was a brave and independent character.*[85]

Tragically, Pemulwuy's skull remains somewhere in England today, as do the mortal remains of some three thousand other Indigenous Australians.

Following the death of Pemulwuy, a period of relative peace returned to the Cumberland Plain, yet with periodic attacks on Aboriginals by white settlers, prompting Judge Advocate David Collins to write, on 27th December 1802, to Under Secretary Sullivan in England:

> *I think there should be an article with instructions, placing the native inhabitants under the protection of the Government, and declaring any violence to their persons or property equally punishable as if offended to a white man.*[86]

Collins' approach to Sullivan, in theory, should not have been necessary for, technically, Aboriginal people were protected as British subjects once the First Fleet had arrived and the territory and its inhabitants had been declared a British possession. Yet, many Aboriginals were shot on sight, sometimes openly, sometimes without being witnessed by or reported to authorities, and sometimes in retaliation for raids on crops, livestock and homes. As with the voice of most moderates, however, Collins' approach to Sullivan passed without response, and white-on-black-on-white violence erupted wherever white settlement intruded on Aboriginal lands throughout other parts of the colony which, by now, was spreading beyond the Sydney-Parramatta-Hawkesbury basin.

White settlement spread to Van Diemen's land in 1803 when Governor King, fearing French settlement in Van Diemen's Land, sent Lieutenant John Bowen to establish a penal colony on the Derwent River, at a site later to be known as Hobart. In 1804, he sent Lieutenant William Paterson to establish another penal colony at Port Dalrymple on the Tamar River. Port Dalrymple would later be named Launceston after the birthplace of Governor Philip Gidley King – Launceston, in Cornwall, England.

In March 1803, Governor King authorised George Howe to establish *The Sydney Gazette & New South Wales*

Advertiser using the government printing press. The *Gazette* quickly became the primary source of information for the settlers, at least for those who could read. The quid pro quo for using the government printing press, of course, was that the *Gazette* was heavily censored, as evidenced by its masthead which carried the wording *Published by Authority*. For many years, almost every issue of the *Gazette* would carry reports speaking in such terms as *"outrageous acts of abominable outrage"* by the natives. The founding of *The Sydney Gazette & New South Wales Advertiser* must bear mention here because, from this point on, it becomes one of the primary sources of information about matters within the colony.

As the maize crops ripened in early 1804, renewed violence broke out on the Cumberland Plain and further north into the lower Hawkesbury between Green Hills and Wisemans Ferry. A Bidjigal warrior known as Tedbury, said to be the son of Pemulwuy, for a time launched sporadic attacks against settlers between George's River and Parramatta. There were reports that Tedbury established something of an attachment to John Macarthur who allowed him to come and go at Elizabeth Macarthur Farm, Parramatta.[87] Tedbury would ultimately be shot and killed by Edward Luttrell at Parramatta, in 1810.[88]

Notwithstanding the ongoing sporadic attacks on the Cumberland Plain, it was further north along the lower Hawkesbury that more sustained and violent Aboriginal resistance broke out. A Darug clan who became known as the Branch Natives launched raids on settlers, their homes and crops and also on river boats on the Hawkesbury. Their homeland was the area around the confluence of the Hawkesbury and the Upper Branch at Lower Portland – the Upper Branch would later be known as the Colo River. Driven to resistance by the loss of their riverbank food sources, the

106

Branch Natives were led by a Darug warrior who became known to the settlers as Branch Jack.

In May 1804, with the maize crop ready for harvest, a raiding party of the Branch Natives attacked the home of Matthew Everingham near Portland Head, spearing Everingham, his wife Elizabeth and their servant, burning their house and out-buildings to the ground and making off with stolen corn cobs and other provisions. Everingham had arrived as a nineteen-year-old convict on the First Fleet and had married Elizabeth Rymes who had arrived as a sixteen-year-old convict on the Second Fleet. At the time of the attack, they had five children, the oldest of whom was eleven and the youngest eighteen months. Everingham, his wife, and his servant survived the spearing and the natives paid no attention to the children, not harming them in any way.

The *Sydney Gazette & New South Wales Advertiser* reported this attack in its issue on 3rd June 1804:

> *We are concerned to state that a few of the natives have again manifested an inclination to hostility, and already proceeded to acts of abominable outrage. Report at the present juncture confines their ravages and barbarity to Portland Head, where Mr Matthew Everingham, settler, his wife, and a servant are said to have been speared; as is also Mr John Howe, settler, near the above spot. The house and out-houses of the former were plundered and afterwards set on fire, but the spear wounds received are not accompanied with any mortal appearance. Several other settlers in this neighbourhood have suffered very considerably in being robbed of their cloathing [sic], flock and grain. On Thursday evening, shortly after the accounts arrived, His Excellency dispatched a file of Troopers to the Magistrate at Hawkesbury, with instructions promptly to adopt such measures as the exigency of the case required. The settlers and constables of that settlement went to the succour of the other settlers at Portland Head; as no*

provocation appears to have been given the Natives in that quarter, and as the Natives in the other districts are still on the domesticated footing they have been for the last two years, it is hoped the exertions that [sic] are making to keep them in that state will have the desired effect, without proceeding to further extremities.[89]

The following week, a party of fourteen armed Hawkesbury settlers, intent on retribution, tracked down a group of some three hundred Darug people, believed to have been those responsible for the attacks on the Everingham and Howe farms. Spears were thrown and the settlers opened fire on the natives. It is not known how many of the natives were killed, but the settlers returned to Richmond Hill with a considerable amount of stolen goods retrieved from the natives.

The *Gazette* report concludes:

Late accounts state that they still continue their ravages, and that another European had been speared at the beginning of the week. Two of the most violent and ferocious were shot at the Green Hills by the Military detachment sent to the relief of the settlers, whose self-preservation requires that they should ever be on the alert to counteract the mischievous designs of the savage and unfeeling enemy.[90]

In late 1804, Governor King, wanting to reach a peaceable arrangement with the Darug people, sent for some of them to meet with him at Parramatta. Three Darug elders agreed to come to Parramatta to discuss their grievances with the Governor, who thereafter wrote to Lord Hobart, Secretary of State for War and the Colonies, telling him of what appeared at the time to be an agreement for more peaceful relations ahead:

…three of the natives from that part of the river readily came on being sent for. On questioning the cause of their disagreement with

the new settlers they very ingenuously answered that they did not like to be driven from the few places that were left on the banks of the river, where alone they could procure food; that they had gone down the river as the white men took possession of the banks. If they went across white men's grounds the settlers fired upon them and were angry; that if they could retain some places on the lower part of the river they should be satisfied and would not trouble the white men. The observation and request appear to be so just and so equitable that I assured them no more settlements should be made lower down the river. With that Assurance they appeared well satisfied and promised to be quiet, in which state they continue.[91]

We cannot help but wonder what would have eventuated had the Governor attempted to secure similar agreements in other parts of the colony. The task would have been difficult in the extreme, not least because the Aboriginals, as we have noted, were not all of one people – they were different clans, different nations, with different levels of hostility and different grievances. Probably it would have been difficult, if not impossible, to use the Hawkesbury agreement as a template to secure other agreements to live-and-let-live, but it remains regrettable that efforts were not made. Yet, even in the limited area of the Hawkesbury, King's agreement would not long endure. The promise he had made to the Darug elders was not one he was capable of keeping, even with the best of intentions. Many allocations of land on the best parts of the river downstream, had already been granted to settlers, some of whom had not yet occupied their land. When they did so, the Darug considered it a breaking of their agreement with the Governor. Furthermore, white settlement along the river was now taking on a life of its own, spreading like a large ink-stain on blotting paper as squatters, with no legal title to land, pegged out their own claims and forced the Darug further off the land King had promised them. It was not long before native hostility along the Hawkesbury recommenced and intensified.

By the beginning of 1805, Branch Jack and his band were becoming increasingly hostile towards settlers along the Hawkesbury. In April 1805, they attacked and killed a settler and former trooper of The New South Wales Corps named John Llewellyn. *The Sydney Gazette & New South Wales Advertiser* reported on it thus:

> *With inexpressible concern we have to recount a series of barbarities lately practised by a banditti of these people, inhabiting the out-skirts of Hawkesbury. Last Wednesday night a fellow known by the name of Branch Jack went to the farm of John Llewellyn, one of the Military settlers, who was at dinner with his labouring servant in a field; he was invited to partake of the fare; and after sharing in the repast, found means to get the settler's musket and powder horn in his possession, with which he made off with a loud yell, which was returned by about 20 others that had before concealed themselves, but now came forward, and discharged several spears at the unfortunate men, two of which entered the master's breast, who fell immediately, two others passing between the servants legs. The latter requesting to know their motive for the barbarous assault, was answered by a flight of spears, one of which penetrated his shoulder, and another one of his groins. After he had fallen the natives closed upon him, and thrice struck him on the head with a tomahawk, each blow occasioning a dreadful wound.*[92]

The same issue of the *Gazette* went on to report on yet another attack by Branch Jack and his band:

> *On the same day another event of the same horrible kind took place at the branch, within three miles of the above. The farmhouse of T. Adlam was set on fire by a body of natives supposed to be the same; and after the alarm had been given, a search was made for the settler and his man, but they had shared*

Less than a week later, the Branch natives attacked the farm of John Cuddy, an Everingham neighbour. Again, *The Sydney Gazette & New South Wales Advertiser* reported the attack:

Last Sunday the natives did considerable damage on Cuddy's farm at Portland Head; and continuing to menace the neighbouring settlers, information was forwarded to the Magistrate at Hawkesbury; who immediately dispatched a party to apprehend if possible the principal aggressors; but the banditti, perhaps apprehensive of their danger, had dispersed before the party arrived.[94]

The next issue of the *Gazette*, on 23rd June 1805 reported yet another attack on a settler's farm, this one belonging to William Knight. The Gazette would go on to report that the natives called out to William Knight by name, perhaps indicating that this was the same William Knight who had earlier been declared an outlaw living with the natives.[95] If this were so, it would appear Knight had surrendered himself and once again returned to the ranks of the colonists.

The natives on Saturday last stripped the farmhouse of William Knight, settler at Boston's Reach Portland Head. At about half past three in the afternoon none were visible, and the settler went with his man into an adjoining field; but were not many paces from the house before they were alarmed with the shouts of a number, who were rushing in at the door, under cover of about a dozen, who with spears shipped, cut off their communication. Branch Jack brought out the settler's musket, and calling him by name, assured him they were by no means apprehensive of the consequences; they then plundered the place, and carried off every article they could find, of bedding, wearing apparel, tea & sugar, meat, and such to an amount which the sufferers declare one hundred pounds sterling would not replace. [96]

Branch Jack was finally brought undone in September 1805 during an audacious attack on a river trading boat, the *Hawkesbury*, belonging to Andrew Thompson, ex-convict and wealthiest settler in the colony, although Thompson was not on board at the time. Confronted on board by musket fire, the Branch warriors dived into the river and attempted to swim ashore, but the crew, firing muskets from the boat, shot several of them, including Branch Jack who died on the banks of the Deerubbin, his ancestral home.

Even without their leader, however, the branch warriors continued their war on the farms of white settlers along the Hawkesbury. Week after week, for more than ten years, virtually every issue of the *Gazette* carried reports of at least one attack during the preceding week. And the *Gazette* made no attempt to humanise the Indigenous people or to suggest they may have some rightful claim to the land they fought for. In various issues of the *Gazette*, the Aboriginals were described as *"savages, villains, barbarous wretches, miscreants, indolent and vicious hordes"* and, in one issue in January 1806, as *"an unhappy race of the least envied beings in existence"*.[97]

In March 1806, King wrote to the Earl of Camden, reporting an attack by Aboriginals on a sealing ship at Twofold Bay (south of present-day Merrimbula).

I am sorry to observe that a small private Colonial vessel laden with seal skins was stranded in Twofold Bay, near the south part of this coast. The natives in great numbers surrounded the few men belonging to the vessel commencing their attack by setting the grass on the surrounding ground on fire and throwing

By 1806, however, Governor King was tiring of the fight, in large measure because of his declining health. Towards the end of his tenure as Governor, King became morbidly obese and was suffering from severe gout and severe fatigue, almost certainly because of poor diet. His mental health also deteriorated, making him angry, pompous and irascible. Believing he had done all he could, both to end the commercial dominance of the Corps and to achieve peace between the settlers and the Indigenous peoples, King had been requesting that he be relieved of his position and a new Governor appointed. Accordingly, the Colonial Office in London appointed Captain William Bligh RN to be the new Governor of the colony. Bligh arrived in Sydney on 6th August 1806 on board *HMS Porpoise*. His term of office would be relatively short.

As King was boarding the *Buffalo* on 15th August 1806 for the voyage to England, he collapsed both physically and mentally, delaying his departure and that of the *Buffalo* until 10th February 1807. As he prepared to sail to England in 1807, King penned a long memo to the new Governor, William Bligh, offering his advice and the wealth of his experience learned as Governor of New South Wales. King's long letter of advice covered many areas of life and administration within the colony, including a section dealing with the natives. King reported to Bligh that he had always endeavoured to maintain peace with the Aboriginals, whom he had *"ever considered the real*

Proprietors of the Soil".[99] He went on to say that he had not allowed the natives to be worked as slaves but that, like former governors, he had failed to understand their ingratitude for the magnanimous benefits being offered them by the more advanced colonial society.[100]

King appears to have been an able and conscientious administrator, even towards the end when he was clearly unwell, and we can well imagine him, sitting in his cabin on *Buffalo* as it ploughed through turbulent seas on the long voyage back to England, reflecting on the turbulence of his own times as Governor of a colony which he had now passed to the hands of another. We get the impression, too, from many of his reports and letters, that he felt some empathy for the plight of the natives and the stand-out phrase from his letter of advice to Bligh was that he, King, considered the natives to be *"the real proprietors of the soil".* It was an incredibly important statement, one never voiced before, and it raises the question of how genuinely, and for how long, King had considered the natives to be *"the real proprietors of the soil".* If that conviction was genuine, how did he reconcile it with his duty, as Governor, to drive the natives away from white settlements *"by firing upon them"?*[101] How did he reconcile a personal, moral conviction that the Aboriginals had a right to the land, as *"the real proprietors of the soil",* whilst working in a role predicated upon the policy of *terra nullius?* Did it torture his mind? We really do not know and can only wish King had said more on this matter.

It should also be acknowledged, of course, that this statement by King might possibly have arisen from his mental state during the time he was preparing for departure and might not actually have been written with a lucid mind. Nonetheless, if genuine, it was indeed an amazing statement to be made by the departing Governor.

The new Governor, William Bligh, arrived at a time which coincided with something of a lull in Aboriginal resistance and hostility, which was just as well for Bligh had his hands full with other matters. In January 1806, little over six months before the arrival of Governor Bligh, the Hawkesbury had been devastated by the worst flooding in white memory. Lives had been lost, farms swept away and many destitute farmers simply gave up and walked off their farms which, in itself, perhaps contributed to the lull in native hostility. One of Governor Bligh's first initiatives on assuming office was to use the colony's stores and herds to provide some relief to farmers who had been severely impacted by the devastation of the Hawkesbury flooding. Supplies to Hawkesbury farmers were allocated on a needs basis, with those unable to pay being granted loans issued by the government. Those humanitarian efforts by Bligh, however, disrupted the barter economy in the colony based on the trade in rum, thus antagonising the Rum Corps who had been exploiting the farmers and profiteering from their dire situation. Throughout 1806 and 1807, therefore, Bligh's efforts were spent fighting not the natives or the convicts, but the officers within the ranks of his own military forces.

Bligh had come to the colony with a determination to bring the officers of the NSW Corps to heel by curbing their privileges and putting an end to their exploitation and corruption. A strong-willed man, as evidenced by his experience when the crew of his ship, *HMS Bounty*, had mutinied in the South Pacific and set him and some loyalists afloat in a small open boat, Bligh had been specifically appointed Governor of the colony because of his reputation as a strong disciplinarian. He had been given full authority by the Colonial Office in London to do whatever necessary to end the Corps' dominance and manipulation of the colony's economy by exercising total control over all trade, by establishing such laws and regulations as he might see fit in relation to the sale of rum and by implementing strong penalties against illegal importation. In every one of those efforts, Bligh came up against the self-interests of John Macarthur and the officers of the Corps who were also angered because Bligh refused to award further large land grants to those who were already wealthy landholders. It was the makings of a serious conflict between Macarthur, aided and abetted by the officers of the Corps, and the Governor, and Bligh was not the kind of man to back down. True to his reputation, Bligh was no respecter of persons and had quickly made enemies of some of the most influential people in the colony.

Macarthur and his cronies in the Rum Corps railed constantly against Bligh and looked for any opportunity to have him removed. In December 1807, Bligh ordered the arrest of Macarthur and charged him with assisting in the escape of a convict on his schooner, *Parramatta*. The judiciary consisted of six officers of the NSW Corps, a legacy of the militarisation of the judiciary that had been instituted by Lieutenant-General Francis Grose in 1793 during the period of military rule. True to form, the six officers of the judiciary dismissed the case against Macarthur, leaving the Judge Advocate unable to proceed. Bligh was incensed and accused the six officers of mutiny.

On 26th January 1808, Bligh again attempted to have Macarthur arrested. Macarthur appealed to his crony, Major George Johnston, Commander of the NSW Corps, who then marched almost the entire Corps, complete with military marching band, to Government House where, under direction from Macarthur, he arrested Governor William Bligh in an act of treason which became known as the Rum Rebellion. Bligh and his widowed daughter, Mary Putland, were held under arrest in Government House, while Macarthur and his lackey,

116

Johnston, declared the military had assumed control of the colony to end the tyrannical, despotic and inept rule of a man unfit to govern.

Johnston promoted himself to Lieutenant-Colonel and assumed the post of Lieutenant-Governor of the Colony of New South Wales. It was twenty years to the day, almost to the hour, since Arthur Phillip had raised the English flag at Sydney Cove. It was also the only time, and would remain the only time, a military coup would change an Australian government. For almost two years until the arrival of a new Governor, a military rebel junta under Lieutenant-Colonel Johnston, Lieutenant-Colonel Joseph Foveaux and Lieutenant-Colonel William Paterson would govern the colony.

Finally, on 28th December 1809, the storeship *Dromedary*, escorted by *HMS Hindostan*, arrived at Port Jackson. On board was the newly appointed Governor of New South Wales, Major-General Lachlan Macquarie, and the newly formed 73rd Regiment of Foot which would replace the NSW Corps. In an inauguration ceremony at Sydney's Government House on New Year's Day 1810, Lachlan Macquarie was sworn in as the fifth Governor of the Colony of New South Wales.

7

TRANSITION
1810 – 1821

Major General Lachlan Macquarie, the first non-naval officer appointed to the governorship of the Colony of New South Wales, was to be the last of the colony's authoritarian governors. He would be responsible for extensive building and infrastructure development within Sydney and the broader colony and would introduce social and economic reforms which played a crucial role in transitioning New South Wales from a penal colony to a free settlement – free for whites that is.

So extensively did his presence permeate the colony during the eleven years of his tenure that, to many white Australians, his name is almost synonymous with the State of New South Wales. The Indigenous people largely take a different view and consider Macquarie a mass murderer. Yet, black or white, it is hard to get away from Macquarie in New South Wales today, for reminders of him are everywhere, including:

- His statue standing prominently at the northern entrance to Sydney's Hyde Park, facing Macquarie Street, one of the principal streets of the Sydney Central Business District (CBD) and home to the NSW State Parliament
- Macquarie Place, a small, historic park in the Sydney CBD
- Mrs Macquarie's Chair, a seat commissioned by Lachlan Macquarie for his wife Elizabeth and carved from a sandstone rock ledge by convicts in 1810. It is a present-day tourist attraction and sits at what is

now the north-eastern end of the Royal Botanic Garden in Sydney, commanding a perfect view of Sydney Cove

- Port Macquarie, a substantial city on the mid-north coast of NSW
- Lake Macquarie, a large inlet on the central coast of NSW
- Macquarie Pass, a mountain route over the escarpment between the Illawarra district and the inland southern highlands of NSW
- Macquarie Lighthouse, Australia's first and longest operating lighthouse
- Macquarie Pier at the mouth of the Hunter River at the port of Newcastle, linking Nobbys Head to the mainland at South Head (now Fort Scratchley)
- The Macquarie River, a major inland river in New South Wales, passing through Bathurst, Wellington, Dubbo and Warren before emptying into the Macquarie Marshes
- The Lachlan River, main tributary of the Murrumbidgee River, rising in the Southern Tablelands of NSW and flowing through Cowra, Forbes and Condobolin
- Mount Macquarie, formerly Mount Lachlan, highest point on the Blainey Plain west of Bathurst
- The Division of Macquarie, one of the first 75 Divisions of the Australian House of Representatives created for the Australian Parliament in 1901
- Macquarie Island, between Tasmania and Antarctica
- The five "Macquarie towns" – Windsor, Wilberforce, Pitt Town, Richmond and Castlereagh, all established by Macquarie on higher ground after the disastrous flooding of the Hawkesbury in 1809

- Macquarie churches, scattered throughout the state of New South Wales and beyond.

The list goes on within present-day New South Wales and beyond – Canberra has a suburb named Macquarie, near Newcastle there is one named Macquarie Hills, and Sydney has the suburbs of Macquarie Links and Macquarie Park.

One of the major thoroughfares in Hobart, Tasmania, is named Macquarie Street and the city also has a suburb known as Macquarie Point. Tasmania has a Macquarie River in the Midlands district, a Macquarie Harbour on the west coast, a town of Lachlan west of Glenorchy and a suburb of Lachlan in the city of Launceston.

Then there are the numerous institutions named after Lachlan Macquarie, including:

- Macquarie University, Sydney
- Macquarie Community College, Western Sydney
- Macquarie Grammar School, Sydney
- Macquarie Hospital, Sydney
- Macquarie Bank and Investment Group
- Macquarie Correctional Centre, a maximum security prison in Wellington NSW.

With all of that, one might be forgiven for thinking Governor Lachlan Macquarie was something of a messiah or at least a saint. Yet, it must be said that, if he was a saint of any kind, it was certainly not a self-deprecating one for many of the places listed above were founded by Macquarie which he then, in all humility, named after himself.

Perhaps he was a saint in the eyes of some, but others were and are aware there was a more nefarious side to

Macquarie. Some metaphoric tarnishing of his statue is evident for those who care to look hard enough.

When they arrived in Sydney in 1809, Lachlan and Elizabeth Macquarie brought with them their Indian slave-servant, a young man named George Jarvis, who, in 1795 at the age of six, had been purchased for 160 rupees in the slave market in Cochin on the Malabar coast of India. Initially, Macquarie had two such slave boys, but the other, whom they had named Hector, had either absconded or been kidnapped in 1799. George had been given a sound education by Macquarie and, by 1801, was no longer considered a slave but rather Macquarie's valet. He arrived on *Dromedary* as Macquarie's senior domestic servant and for almost twelve years had a first-hand view of Macquarie's governorship. Few, however, knew of George's true origins.

Governor Lachlan Macquarie also spent his time in the colony amassing considerable personal wealth. Almost from the moment of his arrival in the colony, the new Governor had sought out and befriended Andrew Thompson, an emancipated convict who was, at that point in time, the wealthiest settler in the colony – the same Andrew Thompson who in 1805, as Chief Constable, had led a team to massacre eight Darug Aboriginals, including the tribal leader, Yaraguwayi.[101] The *Sydney Gazette & New South Wales Advertiser* reported that the Thompson-led expedition had been assisted by native guides *"with a contempt of their brethren and with no other desire of reward than a promise of being permitted to seize and retain a wife a-piece."* [102]

Whether Macquarie's interest in and befriending of Andrew Thompson was because he was a fellow Scot, whether it was because Thompson had not been supportive of the rebel government of Johnston et-al although he had clearly benefited from that regime, whether it was because of his knowledge of and familiarity with the business affairs of the

122

colony, or whether it was purely a pecuniary reason is unclear. Perhaps it was all of those things. Many, however, believed it was the latter.

On 14th January 1810, Macquarie appointed Thompson to the position of Justice of the Peace and Chief Magistrate of the Hawkesbury. It was the first time an ex-convict had been placed in a position of such authority. As Magistrate, Thompson had authority to order imprisonment and/or flogging of those who transgressed the law, be they convicts, emancipated ex-convicts or free-born settlers. The relationship between Thompson and the Governor grew tighter every day and, whenever Andrew Thompson was in Sydney, he was invited to dine with Lachlan and Elizabeth Macquarie at Government House.

Andrew Thompson, however, was in declining health, in large measure because of his heroic efforts in and on the Hawkesbury waters during the floods of 1806 and 1809 when he used his ships to rescue many stranded settlers. He died at his Red House Farm in Green Hills on 22nd October 1810 at only 37 years of age. Thompson had been unmarried and without descendants and, in his will, had bequeathed twenty-five percent of his very extensive estate to his friend, Governor Lachlan Macquarie, who three years later would place a large and wordy memorial headstone on Andrew Thompson's grave.

Perhaps in an attempt to legitimise what by that time had become Macquarie's ever-increasing wealth within the colony and to offer some sense of transparency, the long wording on Thompson's memorial headstone includes a statement relating to Thompson's bequest to the Governor:

In consequence of Mr. Thompson's good conduct, Governor Macquarie appointed him Justice of the Peace. This act, which restored him to that rank in society which he had lost, made so

In 1812, Macquarie ordered production of the colony's first official currency. Using Spanish silver dollar coins, he had the centres cut out of the coins to produce a doughnut styled coin which was then stamped as legal currency of the colony, valued at five shillings a piece. The centre plug cut from the coins, known as the dump, circulated with a value of fifteen pence. Two centuries later, the Macquarie Bank and Investment Group would use the image of one of Macquarie's doughnut coins as its logo.

Under Macquarie, extensive new areas of the colony were opened up by exploration in the Hunter Valley, Port Stephens, Jervis Bay and Van Diemen's Land. Then, in 1813, he sponsored the expedition of Gregory Blaxland, William Wentworth and William Lawson who became the first Europeans to cross the Blue Mountains, opening up beyond the mountains, extensive plains never before seen by non-Indigenous eyes. Once the mountains had been crossed, Macquarie sponsored George Evans to explore the plains beyond, leading to the discovery of a river which was then named the Macquarie River. A year later, Macquarie ordered the establishment of the colony's first inland settlement town, on the Macquarie River and named it Bathurst. The surrounding area became known as the Bathurst Plains. In 1815, Evans found and explored another river in the south-western part of the colony which became known as the Lachlan River.

Surveyor-General, John Oxley, was sent out to explore the area of the Lachlan River in an expedition that opened up huge tracts of prime agricultural land in an area to become known as the Liverpool Plains, bordered to the east by the Great Dividing Range, to the south by the Liverpool Range and to the west by the Warrumbungle Range. The Liverpool

Plains is now occupied by the cities and towns of Tamworth, Werris Creek, Gunnedah, Narrabri, Quirindi and Willow Tree. From the Liverpool Plains, Oxley explored eastwards to the north coast of New South Wales where he found a fine coastal inlet which was then named Port Macquarie. By 1816, exploration, settlement and agriculture had reached deep inland into the colony beyond Bathurst and along the coastline both north and south.

All these incursions of the colony into Aboriginal land, of course, led to further dispossession as the Indigenous peoples were continually pushed away from their ancestral lands and food sources, particularly in the river areas, which must lead to a study of Macquarie's policies towards the Indigenous peoples.

Macquarie had arrived in the colony at the end of 1809, charged with instructions relating to the Indigenous peoples which showed little difference, if any at all, to those given to his four predecessors:

> *You are to endeavour by every possible means to extend your intercourse with the Natives and to conciliate their affections, enjoining all our subjects to live in amity and kindness with them. …you will endeavour to procure from time to time accounts of the numbers of natives inhabiting the neighbourhood of our said settlement and report your opinion to one of our Secretaries of State in what manner the intercourse with these people may be turned to the advantage thereof.*[104]

Governor Lachlan Macquarie, fifth Governor of the Colony of New South Wales, like his four predecessors, hoped and expected to have friendly and peaceful relations with the Indigenous population and, on 1ˢᵗ January 1810, speaking at his swearing in as Governor of the colony, had expressed the wish that Aboriginals should be treated with *"kindness and attention so as to conciliate them as much as possible to our Government and Manners.*"[105] Kind words, but again, words indicative of the colonialist, innate view of their own superiority and right to rule — *"to conciliate them as much as possible to our Government"* can hardly be read with any other interpretation than to put the natives in a position of subservience to the white government.

Fortunately for Macquarie, for perhaps the first four years of his governorship there was seemingly little conflict between the white colonialists/settlers and the Indigenous peoples. Yet by 1814, trouble was again brewing on the Cumberland Plain, centred on the settlement of Appin. During the years 1808-1810, the rebel administration of Johnston, Foveaux and Paterson had issued almost 47,000 acres in settlers' grants, dispossessing the Aboriginal peoples of large swathes of land, which resulted in violent clashes with the white settlers. Not all settlers lived in enmity with the Aboriginals on or near their land. Some endeavoured to co-exist with them, even sometimes displaying a willingness to share part of their crops with them. Professor Grace Karskens writes that although good relations and mutual assistance were common between settlers and Aboriginal people, violence almost always flared as a result of dispossession, the loss of food sources, the taking of Aboriginal women and children, assaults and shootings.[106]

When violence erupted in 1814 between the Aboriginals and the white settlers on the Cumberland Plain, Macquarie's first response was fair and judicial. He launched a magistrates' enquiry which found that the settlers and their convict workers were to blame for the initial aggression (for which payback was carried out) and for escalating the hostilities to a revenge attack on an Aboriginal camp by night. He warned the colonists not to take the law into their own hands and reminded them that the Aboriginal people were protected under British law. He urged forbearance and suggested they share some of their crops with the Aboriginal people.[107]

As relations deteriorated from 1814 onwards, Macquarie made increased attempts to maintain peace through co-operative dialogue, persuasion and assimilation. His efforts during this time included the establishment of The Native Institution in Parramatta for the education of Indigenous children, an invitation to friendly dialogue between the colonists and the Indigenous peoples, and the honouring of those whom he saw as tribal chiefs. All three of those initiatives will shortly be considered in greater detail. Yet, when those efforts failed, he would turn to the use of military force. Yes, he wanted peace with the natives, and would initiate and engage in efforts designed to peacefully assimilate them into white society, but the peace he sought would be peace on his terms, for the precepts and the objectives of colonial policy were not negotiable.

On 7th October 1814, Macquarie sent an extensive report with numerous attached notes to Earl Bathurst, Secretary of State for the Colonies. Macquarie's dispatch included many attachments and was a general description of the state of the colony, including a short report concerning relations with the Indigenous people:

> *I have great pleasure in reporting to Your Lordship that this country is at present in a state of perfect peace and tranquillity. In my former dispatch I had to notice some sanguinary acts on the part of the natives but since that period they have entirely discontinued their predator incursions and savage attacks on the settlers… It has long been in Serious contemplation with me to endeavour to civilize the Aborigines of this country so as to render them industrious and useful to the government, and at the same time to improve their own condition. Having made some*

In his attached note (Note 70), Macquarie suggested to Bathurst that the Aboriginals whom he saw as people *"scarcely emerged from the remotest state of rude and uncivilized nature"* might be changed from their *"wretched and destitute state"* and could perhaps become useful to the colony *"either as labourers in agricultural employ or among the lower class of mechanics"*.[109] Such comments leave little cause to doubt the demeaning manner in which Macquarie viewed the Indigenous people. He then went on to outline his somewhat pretentious and patronising plans to establish an educational Institution for Indigenous children:

> *From considerations of this kind, which in a great measure have been guided and strengthened by my own personal knowledge and observation, I have determined to make an experiment towards the civilization of these natives, which is the object I have in view by this address and trust it will meet your Lordship's benevolent Patronage. As a preliminary Measure I intend to establish an Institution at Parramatta, first on a small scale under the direction of a Mr William Shelley (formerly a missionary), whom I shall appoint as superintendent for educating and bringing up to habits of industry and decency the youth of both sexes, commencing at the outset with six boys and six girls.*[110]

The submission included a budget estimate of annual costs for establishing and operating the institution at Parramatta, submitted by said Mr Shelley[111] – this, of course being the issue Macquarie referred to when seeking Bathurst's *"benevolent patronage"*.

Bathurst approved Macquarie's plan to establish the Native Institution, albeit seemingly with some scepticism about the success of the project, and the institution opened in

January 1815. Approximately forty Indigenous children passed through the Institution before its closure in 1823. Macquarie viewed it as a humanitarian endeavour to civilise the natives and in many ways it was, with a number of Aboriginal children gaining some level of education and thereafter improving their place in Sydney's white society. One such student was Maria Lock, daughter of Yarramundi, chief of the Darug people. Maria went on to be recognised as the matriarch of the Darug people of Western Sydney, although that was more likely because of her kinship to Yarramundi rather than a result of the education she had gained in the Native Institution.

Notwithstanding the fact that Macquarie no doubt considered the establishment of the Native Institution to be a noble and benevolent exercise, there are a couple of issues of concern which arise when viewed from twenty-first century perspectives. In his Government and General Order of 10th December 1814, Macquarie made it quite clear that *"the main objective of the Institution shall be the Civilization of the Aborigines of both sexes."*[112]

As part of that civilising process, Indigenous children would be removed from their families, sometimes forcibly and sometimes "found" separated from their parents during frontier conflicts. The children would be taught to read and write (English, of course), to recite Bible scriptures and to calculate simple arithmetic. Additionally, the girls would be taught domestic duties and needlework, preparing them for household servant duties while the boys would learn farming techniques and elementary maintenance of machinery. All very laudable endeavours in Macquarie's view but, overall, a curriculum designed to civilise the children through forced assimilation and loss of their Aboriginal language, culture, and heritage.

Reinforcing the civilising objectives of the curriculum was the nature of the Institution itself and the age of children to be admitted. This was not to be a native school, where children could attend each day and return to their families each evening. Rather, it was to be a children's home and asylum run by a Christian missionary, William Shelley, for those children *"separated from their families"*. Children, once admitted, would be permanent residents within the Institution. This fact, combined with the tender age of the students, gives rise to some serious areas of concern. Macquarie's General Order establishing the institution contained specific clauses relating to these issues:

> *Sixthly, That this Institution shall be an Asylum for the Native Children of both sexes, but no child shall be admitted under four, or exceeding seven years of age.*[113]

and

> *Fourteenthly, That no child, after having been admitted into the Institution, shall be permitted to leave it, or be taken away by any person whatever (whether Parents or other Relatives) until such time as the boys shall have attained the age of sixteen years, and the girls fourteen years; at which ages they shall be respectively discharged.*[114]

Indigenous children, therefore, would be totally removed from their families and culture, most often forcibly, for a period of between ten to twelve years. Some native children were solicited from their parents, perhaps under duress and under varying levels of intoxication, and others were seized during frontier conflict. The practice of government authorities removing Aboriginal children from their families to educate them in the ways of western civilisation, as occurred at the Native Institution, whilst perhaps well intentioned, was in many ways an earlier manifestation of another assimilation project which in the twentieth century would come to be known as the Stolen

130

Generation. Some contemporary historians see Macquarie's Institution as a social experiment, controlling and reshaping the lives of Aboriginal children. Patricia Hale and Tanya Koeneman write that young boys and girls were raised together to be married off to each other and settled on small farms to raise their own Christian children and produce food for the colony, just as the small-landholding ex-convict settlers were expected to do.[115]

While preparations were still underway for establishing the Native Institution, Macquarie issued an invitation to all Aboriginals in the Parramatta district to attend a friendly dialogue at the Parramatta marketplace on 28th December 1814. Macquarie viewed it as a means of exerting his authority without force and, in particular, by offering friendly dialogue, food and drink (alcoholic), to induce Aboriginal parents to give up their children to his benevolent Native Institution. The Parramatta conferences became annual events and were the primary means of recruiting children to the Institution.

The *Sydney Gazette & New South Wales Advertiser* reported on the inaugural conference thus:

On Wednesday, HIS EXCELLENCY the Governor went to Parramatta, for the purpose of seeing and conferring with the Natives, agreeably to the benevolent design intimated in the General Orders of the 10th instant. At one o'clock HIS EXCELLENCY, accompanied by the LIEUTENANT GOVERNOR, and a number of Officers Civil and Military, went to the marketplace, where the interview had been appointed to be held, and conversed with them for an hour, pointing out in an affable and familiar way the advantages they would necessarily derive from a change of manners and an application to moderate industry. The whole number assembled, of all ages and sexes, did not exceed sixty, owing, as it was conjectured, to some false impressions with the more distant tribes had given way to, relative to the design of the convocation, suspiciously imagining that they were to be forcibly deprived of their children and themselves sent to labour. After a length of conversation, three children were yielded up to the benevolent purposes of the institution; and after HIS EXCELLENCY, His Honor the LIEUTENANT GOVERNOR and the accompanying officers had bestowed every possible pains in producing a confidence necessary to the proposed ends, the natives were seated in a circle, and served with a fine dinner of roast beef, and a cheering jug of ale.[116]

On the occasion of the second such annual conference, Macquarie invoked a practice of rewarding Aboriginals who had assisted the British, by arbitrarily declaring them to be chiefs of their respective tribes. Macquarie's 'chiefs' were presented with a gorget (a brass breastplate) engraved with their name and the name of their tribe and declaring them to be the chief of said tribe.

At Macquarie's annual conferences, providing the Aboriginals with alcoholic drink appears to have been part of a strategy designed to bring about a general feeling of bonhomie amongst them. The annual reporting of the conferences by the *Sydney Gazette & New South Wales Advertiser* invariably made mention of the alcohol provided to the Aboriginals:

On Saturday last the 28th. ult. the Town of Parramatta exhibited a novel and very interesting spectacle by the assembling of the Native Tribes there, pursuant to the GOVERNOR'S gracious invitation. …The natives having seated themselves on the ground in a large circle. … In the centre of the circle thus formed, were placed large tables groaning under the weight of roast beef, potatoes, bread, &c. and a large cask of grog lent its exhilarating aid to promote the general festivity and good humour which so conspicuously shone through the sable visages of this delighted congress.[117]

As Aboriginal resistance to the spread of white settlement increased, there was a corresponding hardening of Macquarie's attitudes and responses towards the Aboriginal peoples. In March 1816 near Mulgoa, Aboriginal warriors speared and killed four settlers, It seems to have been at this point that Macquarie reverted to his persona as a ruthless military commander. He responded by sending out three detachments of troops into all parts of the Cumberland Plain, to *"Punish the Hostile Natives, by clearing the Country of them entirely"*.[118]

Because the Aboriginal children being "civilised" within the Native Institution were always few in number, Macquarie also instructed his officers to bring back twelve boys and six girls between four and six years of age for the Native Institution – *"but only fine, healthy and good-looking children"*[119] so that his showpiece Native Institution could continue to operate. As it eventuated, the troops were able to capture only two boys, both of whom absconded from the Institution within a few weeks.[120]

On Wednesday, 10th April 1816, Macquarie wrote in his journal:

> *I have this Day ordered three Separate Military Detachments to march into the Interior and remote parts of the Colony, for the purpose of Punishing the Hostile Natives, by clearing the Country of them entirely, and driving them across the mountains.*

> *In the event of the Natives making the smallest show of resistance – or refusing to surrender when called upon so to do – the officers Commanding the Military Parties have been authorized to fire on them to compel them to surrender; hanging up on Trees the Bodies of such Natives as may be killed on such occasions, in order to strike the greater terror into the Survivors.*[121]

The three military detachments set out that same day, 10th April 1816. One detachment led by Captain Schaw went to the Hawkesbury where he and his men failed to find a single Aboriginal. Lieutenant William Dawes led another detachment to the Cowpastures and found himself on the Macarthur estate where two Aboriginal warriors were killed and one boy taken prisoner. Captain James Wallis led his detachment south-west to the districts of Airds and Appin.

Acting on a tip-off that there was an Aboriginal encampment above the Cataract Gorge, Wallis took his troops on an overnight march towards Appin. They arrived to find the campsite abandoned, but hot embers in fireplaces at the campsite and the cry of a baby gave evidence of the Aboriginals being nearby. Wallis reported that he formed "line rank entire", a continuous line of soldiers side by side, and pushed through the thick bush until they came upon the natives. The soldiers opened fire and bayoneted Aboriginal men, women and children, driving others over the high cliffs and into the gorge of the Cataract River. At least fourteen Aboriginal men, women and children were killed in the massacre and, in accordance with Macquarie's orders, Aboriginal corpses were hung in trees *"in order to strike the greater terror into the Survivors"*. By these words, Macquarie's own words, he defines himself as a terrorist.

Macquarie produced a defence of the massacre by stating only that *"several natives have been unavoidably killed and wounded"* and going on to claim that they were themselves to blame because they had not surrendered themselves on being called to do so.[122] But, contrary to Macquarie's orders, the Aboriginal people had not been called upon to surrender. In his report to Earl Bathurst, Secretary of State for the Colonies, in England, Macquarie again falsely asserted that the Aboriginal people had resisted the soldiers. He also omitted

134

the fact that the five prisoners taken were women and children.[123]

The Appin massacre is often said to have marked the end of Aboriginal hostilities on the Cumberland Plain. It may have been the beginning of the end, yet it unleashed another spate of violence and killings and a long campaign of retributive raids which would continue until the end of 1816. James Wallis was rewarded for his role in the Appin Massacre when Macquarie appointed him to be the Commandant of the Newcastle penal colony.

In London, however, Macquarie's administration of the colony was earning increasing disapproval, not because of his dealings with the natives but largely because of his policy of emancipating convicts and also the lavish amounts being spent on public works. The British government still viewed New South Wales as little else than a penal colony and therefore a place to serve as a disincentive to unlawful acts in England, rather than a new and free life for convicts in a new land. Macquarie's efforts to make New South Wales a place of reform for convicts rather than simply a place of punishment was viewed, in London, as misguided. In 1819, John Bigg, an English judge, was sent to New South Wales to report on Macquarie's administration.

In New South Wales, Bigge was influenced by large landholders such as Archibald Bell, Samuel Marsden, John Macarthur and others who wanted convict labour to be withdrawn from Macquarie's urban building works and assigned exclusively to work on their large land holdings.[124] Bigge was swayed and believed that government expenditure in the colony could be significantly decreased through reassignment of convicts and a corresponding decrease in government building projects. Additionally, Bigge believed, the Australian wool output and, in turn, the British wool industry, would benefit from the reassignment of convicts as free labour to the large pastoralists.[125]

The acrimony between Macquarie and Bigge led to Macquarie's resignation which was accepted in 1820. Thomas Brisbane replaced him as Governor in 1821, though the departure of Lachlan and Elizabeth Macquarie was delayed until February 1822. The *Surry* sailed from Port Jackson, bound for England, on 12th February 1822 with Lachlan Macquarie on board – the last authoritarian Governor of the Colony of New South Wales. A little over a year into Thomas Brisbane's tenure, the New South Wales Act 1823 established the colony's first legislative body to advise the Governor, the New South Wales Legislative Council.

The plaque on Lachlan Macquarie's mausoleum on the Isle of Mull, Scotland, declares him to be *"The Father of Australia."*

In front of his statue in Sydney's Hyde Park, a large metal plaque set into the footpath carries a glowing eulogy, including the words, *"He was a perfect gentleman, a Christian and supreme legislator of the human heart. His government was more ratified by his own merits than by his official insignia and whenever the sculptor shall imagine a guardian angel for New South Wales and Van Diemen's Land, the chisel of gratitude shall portray the beloved and majestic features of General Macquarie."*

Yet almost every year on 26th January, Aboriginal activists and their supporters throw red paint, representing Aboriginal blood, on the Hyde Park statue and frequently daub slogans declaring Macquarie to have been a mass-murderer and an agent of genocide – proof again, if proof is needed, that we are not reconciled, that there are deep divisions between us

136

and that black and white Australians feel very differently about our history. Today, many of those Aboriginal activists want to see Macquarie's statue in Hyde Park torn down.

Professor Bronwyn Carlson is a D'harawal woman from New South Wales, the Head of Indigenous Studies at Macquarie University in Sydney and author of *The Politics of Identity: Who Counts as Aboriginal Today?* [126] Speaking in an interview on the ABC Radio National Breakfast Program on 29th August 2017, Professor Carlson stated that "most Indigenous people" would call for the removal of colonial statues celebrating the massacres and the genocide of Indigenous peoples, particularly the statue of Lachlan Macquarie. The interviewer went on to ask Professor Carlson whether she would be happy to see colonial statues retained but with new plaques better reflecting the Indigenous perspective.

"Well," replied Professor Carlson, "What do you want the plaque to say? Would people be satisfied to say, 'Here stands a mass-murderer who ordered the genocide of Indigenous people'? or perhaps 'Here is a man who ordered Indigenous people to be slaughtered on sight'? Is that the kind of plaque you'd want?"[127]

8

THE KILLING FIELDS

What constitutes a massacre? A legally constituted definition of genocide was determined by the United Nations in 1948 in the wake of the Nazi Holocaust, yet there is no legally accepted definition of a massacre. Most international scholars of ethnic violence agree that the word can legitimately be used to speak of the unlawful killing of six or more people (some use three or more as the criteria) in the same incident over a short period of time and within close proximity to one another.

Professor Lyndall Ryan leads the University of Newcastle's Colonial Frontier Massacres Project Team[128] recording and documenting the massacres of Aboriginal people throughout Australia in the years 1788 – 1930. The research team has produced an online interactive map[129] showing locations and details of more than three hundred massacres of Indigenous peoples across Australia, using the criteria of six or more people being unlawfully killed in one incident. The map is a work in progress and Professor Ryan expects that ultimately, more than four hundred massacres are likely to be documented.

This book was never intended to be a complete litany of killings or massacres across the colony or across the nation post-federation. To have attempted that would have necessitated a much more extensive work, as Professor Ryan's map shows. Yet, it seems pertinent here, to list just a few of the many major massacres, some perpetrated by groups of settlers and by marauding groups of stockmen and others which were officially sanctioned by governments. Colonial newspapers of the time routinely reported the massacre of Indigenous peoples.

West of the Nepean, NSW 1805

The *Sydney Gazette & New South Wales Advertiser* reported on 12 May 1805 the *"successful assault"* which had been conducted against the Branch Natives *"a fortnight since"*, meaning somewhere around 1st May 1805. Mr Andrew Thompson, ex-convict and probably the wealthiest settler in the colony, who would later be appointed to the position of Chief Constable and Magistrate by Governor Lachlan Macquarie, led the attack by a large group of settlers in a mission to "pacify" and "disperse" the Branch Natives. The words "pacify" and "disperse" were frequently used by the *Gazette* as euphemisms meaning to kill. Thompson and his party were assisted by *"a couple of Richmond Hill natives who were entrusted with firelocks to attend as guides, with no other desire of reward than a promise of being permitted to seize and retain a wife a-piece."* The *Gazette* went on to report that "seven or eight" Darug Aboriginals were killed in the attack, including the tribal leader, Yaraguwayi.[130]

Andrew Thompson would later become a close personal friend of Governor Lachlan Macquarie. As noted earlier, he often dined at Government House with the Governor and Mrs Macquarie and would leave 25% of his extensive personal fortune to the Governor in his will. It seems inconceivable that the Governor would not have been aware of Thompson's involvement in this massacre or that he would have allowed a close personal relationship to have developed, including receiving Thompson at his table, without approving of Thompson's past actions.

Van Diemen's Land 1825 – 1832

The Black War was a war waged in Van Diemen's Land, later to be called Tasmania, from 1825 until 1832 and came very close to totally exterminating the Indigenous population of that island. Indeed, debate continues today as to whether the mass-murder of Indigenous people during the Black War should be considered an act of genocide. Lyndall Ryan's analysis of population studies led her to conclude that, at the time of the first British arrivals in 1803, there were about seven thousand Indigenous people spread throughout the island's nine nations.[131]

From 1825 to 1828, a state of open warfare existed between the disparate Indigenous tribes of Van Diemen's land and the white settlers supported by soldiers and field police. Six colonists were murdered by Indigenous raiders between September and November 1826. By the beginning of December 1826, the *Colonial Times* of Hobart was calling for the permanent removal of Aborigines from the island.

> *In conducting a Journal, which is understood to express the general sentiments and wishes of the people, and in some instances, to regulate and lead them, we are occasionally obliged to present those subjects to the attention of our Readers, which the pressing necessity of the case requires, although they may be attended with painful results… we now beg most earnestly, to draw the attention of all, to the present situation of those poor, wretched, but infatuated savages, the Aborigines of this Island. In devoting a few observations to the cause of humanity – in tracing the dangers to which the Settler must be exposed, and in pointing out a remedy, if possible, we are not only doing our duty, as Christians, but as Men; and if we offer any observations which are entitled to weight, it is also the duty, as we are sure it will be the inclination, of Government, to act upon them...*
>
> *It is too late to discuss the question, whether they might not have been civilized… nothing, but a removal, can protect us from incursions, similar to the Caffrees in Africa, or the backwoodsmen, in North America…. they [the settlers] are now exposed to the attack of these natives, who aim at their lives.*

<blockquote>
We make no pompous display of Philanthropy - we say unequivocally, SELF DEFENCE IS THE FIRST LAW OF NATURE. THE GOVERNMENT MUST REMOVE THE NATIVES – IF NOT, THEY WILL BE HUNTED DOWN LIKE WILD BEASTS, AND DESTROYED! ... If they remain here, they are SURE TO BE DESTROYED... We shall hail with joy any measure the Council may devise, to effectually relieve us from this calamity, but they may be assured no half-measures will suffice.[132] (Words in brackets added by the author for clarification.)
</blockquote>

Four months later, two stockmen were killed by Aborigines near Campbell Town in the northern part of the island, and a detachment of the 40th Regiment, supplemented by a number of settlers, killed up to seventy Aboriginal men, women and children in a reprisal attack.

In May 1827, a group of Aboriginal warriors killed another stockman near Swansea at Great Oyster Bay. In retaliation, a large force of soldiers, field police and settlers launched a night raid on an Aboriginal camp. Professor Lyndall Ryan states that "the number slain was considerable".[133]

In June 1827, at least a further one hundred members of the Pallittorre tribe were massacred in reprisal attacks after the killing of three stockmen. Lyndall Ryan calculates that, in the eight months from 1st December 1826 to 31st July 1827, more than two hundred Aboriginal people were killed in the Settled Districts of Van Diemen's Land in reprisal for their killing of up to fifteen colonists. By March 1828, the death toll in the Settled Districts for the previous year and a half had risen to forty-three colonists and probably three hundred and fifty Aboriginal people.[134] Almost certainly, those Indigenous people who were killed in these actions were not the perpetrators of the original violence. They were simply the convenient scapegoats on whom retribution could be taken –

an example of collective punishment of innocents for the acts of others.

In April 1828, Governor Arthur sent a report on what he saw as the Aboriginal problem to the Secretary for the Colonies, William Huskisson, stating his plan to entirely prohibit the Aboriginals from entering the settled districts yet also making it clear that he believed the convicts and the settlers to be the primary cause of the violence.

> *We are undoubtedly the first aggressors, and the desperate characters amongst the prisoner population, who have from time to time absconded into the woods, have no doubt committed the greatest outrages upon the natives, and these ignorant beings, incapable of discrimination, are now filled with enmity and revenge against the whole body of white inhabitants. It is perhaps at this time in vain to trace the cause of the evil which exists; my duty is plainly to remove its effects; and there does not appear any practicable method of accomplishing this measure, short of entirely prohibiting the Aborigines from entering the settled districts.*[135]

In October 1830 Lieutenant-Governor George Arthur ordered the formation of the Black Line – three lines, actually, comprised of soldiers, convicts and free settlers totalling around 2,200 men. They formed a human chain moving southward and attempting to drive all Aboriginal people south and into the confines of the Tasman Peninsula. It was what the *Colonial Times* would have called *"no half measure"*.[136] Yet in many ways it was a failure. By the time the Line was formed, there were not many Aboriginal people left in Van Diemen's Land and gaps in the Line allowed those remaining to slip through and return to their ancestral lands. Only two Aborigines were killed and a further two captured. The Line was disbanded on 26th November 1830. From 1830 onwards, there was little Aboriginal violence in Van Diemen's Land because their numbers had been so decimated. Van Diemen's

Land was renamed Tasmania on 1st January 1956. Since those dark days, the number of Indigenous people living in Tasmania has increased and the 2021 census recorded the number of Tasmanians identifying as Aboriginal or Torres Strait Islanders at 30,186.[137]

Slaughterhouse Creek 26th January 1838

Fifty years to the day after Arthur Phillip raised the British flag at Sydney Cove and declared the Colony of New South Wales, Waterloo Creek, southwest of Moree NSW, became the site of one of the most horrific massacres in NSW. It is thought likely that the fifty-year anniversary of the first landing was used as the pretext for a massacre designed to 'put the natives in their place'. Following the massacre, Waterloo Creek became more appropriately known as Slaughterhouse Creek. There is no definite count of the number of Aboriginals killed, with reports varying between forty and seventy. In October 1899, the *Evening News* (Sydney) reported on the passing of the last surviving Aborigine from that massacre:

> *The death of an old gin, at one of the aboriginal camps in the Gwydir district, who was said to be the last survivor of the blacks who escaped from the slaughter of the natives by some white men in 1838, recalls to mind the details of that coldblooded and deliberate massacre. According to the papers of that period, only one gin escaped, although one witness at the first trial stated that he kept back from the victims who were led out to death one child of about five years old. This may or may not have been the gin who has just died. The facts of the case were simply that the men, assigned servants, went out one Sunday well-armed, went to the camp of some quiet blacks, and drove them into the hut of one Kilmaister, who appears to have been the ringleader in the matter. These blacks had been accustomed to look upon Kilmaister as being, friendly disposed towards them – in fact, a kind of protector. Nevertheless, he led the others on in tying up these*

natives and leading them forth to death. In his summing up at the second trial, Judge Burton said, "In that hut the prisoners [sic], unmoved by the tears, groans, and sighs, bound them with cords, fathers, mothers, and children indiscriminately, and carried them away to a short distance, when the scene of slaughter commenced, and stopped not until all were exterminated. The massacre was atrocious, including as it did babies at their mothers' breasts. The murderers were armed with swords and pistols, and hacked and decapitated the wretched and defenceless natives, then heaped their bodies together, and tried to burn them. Eleven men — Charles Kilmaister, William Hawkins, James Parry, Edward Foley, James Oates, John Russell, John Johnson, J. Blake, C. Toulouse, C. Lamb, and G. Palliser – were put on their trial for this murder and acquitted. Attorney-General Plunkett had the first seven of the above list tried on a separate charge, namely, the murder of an aboriginal black child, name unknown. On this charge the seven men were convicted and hanged.[138]

Myall Creek 1838

Following soon after the massacre at Slaughterhouse Creek, and perhaps inspired by it, was the massacre at Myall Creek station, west of the NSW town of Inverell and southeast of Moree. On 9th June 1838, a group of eleven stockmen, all convicts or ex-convicts, apart from the leader of the group, John Henry Fleming, arrived at the Myall Creek station. They rode up to a gathering of station huts where a group of approximately thirty Aboriginal people of the Kamilaroi Nation sat. When the stockmen rode into their camp, the Aboriginals fled into a convict supervisor's hut, pleading for protection. The convict supervisor asked the raiding stockmen what they intended to do with the Aboriginal people whereupon Fleming replied, "We're going to take them over the back of the range and frighten them." The stockmen then entered the hut, tied the Aboriginals together with a long rope and led them away. They took them to a gully about a thousand yards to the west of the station and there they slaughtered every one of them – at least twenty-eight Aboriginal women, children, and old men.

Testimony was later given at trial that the stockmen had decapitated the children and hacked the men and women to pieces with swords. After the massacre, the group dispersed and Fleming, the only free man involved, disappeared. Though the other members of the gang were ultimately arrested and faced trial on charges of murder, Fleming was never captured. He hid or was protected, probably in the Hawkesbury district, where he later became a respected farmer, church warden and Justice of the Peace. Seven members of the gang were publicly hanged for their part in the crime at Sydney Goal on 18th December 1838.

The trials of the murderers involved in the Myall Creek massacre and the Slaughterhouse Creek massacre surprised white Australians across the nation – they were the first occasions on which white Australians were charged and hanged for killing Aborigines. Until then, many white Australians believed it was not an offence to kill Aboriginal people.

The Coniston Massacre 1928

Coniston cattle station is located in Central Australia about 250 kilometres northwest of Alice Springs. In 1928, a Northern Territory police constable, William Murray, was tasked with investigating the murder of a white stockman, Fred Brooks, by Aborigines near Coniston. From August to October 1928, Murray led punitive raids on local Aboriginal groups, killing, officially, thirty-one Aboriginal people from the Kaytetye and Walpiri nations. Testimonies from Aboriginals who survived the massacre, however, claim that the number of Aboriginals massacred in raids by the Murray task force was between two hundred and three hundred.

Murray later took two Aboriginal prisoners to Darwin to face trial for the killing of Brooks. In court, the two Aboriginal prisoners were acquitted, but it is the testimony of Murray himself which still astounds readers today. In court, Murray openly acknowledged that he had shot a large number of Aboriginals, that he shot to kill and that he shot wounded and dying Aboriginals, leading the judge to note that Murray had "mowed them down wholesale". Following the trial, a government Board of Inquiry was established to investigate Murray's actions. The findings of the Board of Inquiry were that Murray had no case to answer because the shootings were justified.[139] Murray, the Inquiry found, had acted in self-defence. How the killing of wounded and dying people could be considered an act of self-defence was not revealed in court.

The list could go on and on and on.
The Minnamurra River Massacre, NSW (1818)
The Bathurst Massacre, NSW (1824)
The Cape Grim Massacre, Van Diemen's Land (1828)
The Pinjarra Massacre, WA (1833)
The Convincing Ground Massacre, VIC (1833)
The Mount Cottrell Massacre, VIC (1836)
The Mount Dispersion Massacre, NSW (1836)
The Campaspe Plains Massacre, VIC (1839)
The Rufus River Massacre, NSW (1836)
The Wonnerup Massacre, WA (1841)
The Convincing Ground Massacre, VIC (1841)
The Evans Head Massacre, NSW (1842)
The Kilcoy mass-poisoning, QLD (1842)
The Whiteside Station Massacre, QLD (1847)
The East Ballina Massacre, NSW (1854)

The Mistake Creek Massacre, WA (1915)
The Forrest River Massacre, WA (1926)
The Murdering Gully Massacre, VIC (1839)
The Blood Hole Massacre, VIC (1839)
The Fighting Hills Massacre, Hamilton, VIC (1840)
The Warrigal Creek Massacre, VIC (1843)
The Blanket Bay Massacre, Cape Otway, VIC (1840)
The Koonchera Point Massacre, SA (1880)

There are many, many more – hundreds more – too many to list. In addition to the hundreds of documented massacres by shooting or killing with swords, there are also many documented cases of poisoning. Some were investigated by government authorities, but no charges of poisoning were ever pursued. Substances used in mass-poisonings included prussic acid, arsenic, strychnine and corrosive sublimate, all chemicals which became commonly used in agriculture from around 1820.

Many white Australians in the twenty-first century are totally unaware of the vast number of Aboriginal killings that took place in our history. Some acknowledge that "Well, yes, there may have been some killings, maybe even a few massacres". Some have heard of the massacres, spoken of in whispers as part of our shameful history. Some, even when confronted with the documented evidence, simply refuse to believe it happened. Yet the stories do not go away, because they are real. Those Australians who, like me, are proud of their country must also face the reality that this is the history of our land – this is the history we have all inherited.

9

PATHWAY TO RECONCILIATION

Do we turn away from the truth when it shames us? Of course, we do! We all do it. It is a natural instinctive reaction when confronted with our own shame. Often, even in the twenty-first century, white Australians turn away from the Indigenous people themselves. Too often they are looked down on and considered not quite as good as us – or perhaps not nearly as good as us. It is an attitudinal flaw in our psyche, a form of racism that has been inculcated in us since the first colonial days of this country. Most white Australians are yet to break free of it.

Surely, no author could write a book such as this without the belief or at least the hope that reconciliation between our black and white citizens is possible. Numerous commentators, black and white, have advanced what they consider to be the essential requirements and prerequisites for such reconciliation and it would be presumptuous in the extreme for me to think that I could do better – especially to think that I could do better than the Indigenous peoples themselves. Nonetheless, there are some matters which, to me at least, would appear to be important steps towards genuine reconciliation.

Listen rather than talk

The very first point to be made in any consideration of reconciliation is that white Australia must listen to the Indigenous people. For far too long, they have been told what is needed, what our society should look like and how it can be achieved. They have been told that since 1788. It is time to listen – this is the first step in a more complex dialogue that needs to be had between black and white Australians. This dialogue is what Indigenous Australians call a process of "truth telling" and it involves white Australians listening and having the courage to acknowledge the injustices perpetrated against Aboriginal peoples, past and present. It must result in white

Australians reaching out in a spirit of humility and egalitarianism, allowing us all to move forward together with mutual respect.

A national apology

Aboriginal people today feel rightly aggrieved at the way their people have been treated since 26th January 1788, and a genuine apology on the part of the nation must be the first step if this nation is ever going to move forward in a spirit of reconciliation. "Sorry" is one of the hardest words to say yet, if an apology can be made for the Stolen Generation, as Prime Minister Kevin Rudd did on 13th February 2008, then surely the nation can apologise to the Indigenous peoples for the invasion of their land, for the stealing of their women and children, for the massacres and genocide and for all the wrongs perpetrated upon them. That may be difficult for some within the white Australian community, and we probably should not expect 100% of white Australians to embrace such an act of apology any more than we should expect 100% of Indigenous Australians to accept such an apology. Yet that is where a start must be made – a formal apology on the part of the nation and a reaching out to embrace First Nations people by the white community. An apology is long overdue and we cannot move forward without it.

Recognition – public monuments

This country is dotted with monuments memorialising white explorers, white governors, white prime ministers, white pioneer women/families, white British playwrights and poets, white Australian poets, white sculptors and painters, white British sovereigns, white Australian soldiers and war heroes.

Where is the statue of Pemulwuy? Where is the statue of Bennelong? Why is there no statue of Branch Jack? Australians respect and honour their war dead who fought in wars on foreign soil – there are war memorials, statues, and

150

honour rolls to remind the nation of the debts owed to them. Why are there no memorials to those who fought for and on their own land here in Australia? Why are there no commemorations of the wars fought here on Australian soil between the Indigenous people and white colonists? The reason is that history is written and monuments erected by the victors. The vanquished, it is hoped, will fade into obscurity. Even the National War Memorial in Canberra looks the other way on this issue – they really do not want to talk about it. Yet, public statues commemorating the sacrifices of Aboriginal leaders during the Frontier Wars would play an important role, not only by inculcating pride and greater self-esteem in the nation's Indigenous citizens but also by educating white Australians about the causes of the divisiveness in our society.

Education

As a former teacher, I am heartened to see that, in recent years, greater emphasis has been given within our schools' curriculum to Indigenous culture and history. Some schools now have Indigenous names, some expose our children to Indigenous art and culture through music, drama and public murals, etc. One exceptionally pleasing aspect of our education system is that more and more Indigenous Australians are choosing careers in teaching, not only becoming wonderful teachers of Mathematics, Science, Humanities and other subjects but at the same time exposing our children to a broader understanding of Indigenous culture. In our humanities classes, our children, especially in secondary schools, are now being taught about the conflicts between Indigenous peoples and the colonists.

Yet, it is my opinion that even greater emphasis needs be given to the teaching of Indigenous issues and particularly to addressing the racist attitudes that continue to pervade this country. Unless told about the racial divide in this country and its causes, how can young white Australians of this generation and the next be expected to develop an empathy with our Indigenous peoples and an awareness of the injustices perpetrated upon them by our forebears? The story of dispossession and of the ensuing wars between black and white Australians needs to be brought out into the open and discussed with honour, with respect and, where necessary, with shame, as part of the truth telling process. Only then will black and white Australians be able to move forward on an equal footing and in a spirit of true reconciliation. School curriculums across the nation need to include greater emphasis on educating our children about the black-white conflict that arose following white settlement of this country – about the violence perpetrated by both sides in that conflict, about the root causes of that conflict and about the resulting impact of that violence on the psyche of both black and white Australians ever since. Failure to do so perpetuates the divide in our nation and makes us complicit in the treatment of Indigenous Australians by those who have gone before us.

Repatriation

When Pemulwuy was shot and killed in June 1802, he was decapitated and his head, preserved in spirits, was sent like some grotesque souvenir to Sir Joseph Banks in England. Indigenous groups within this country have repeatedly requested the return of Pemulwuy's skull to his Country and to his people, yet the British government and the authorities within British museums have claimed that the skull cannot be found. That is simply not good enough, and the Australian government, even the Australian Prime Minister, should be demanding that greater efforts be made on the part of British authorities to locate the skull and repatriate it to this country. Pemulwuy is a revered figure and a hero amongst Indigenous Australians and it is scandalous that his skull, severed from his

152

body by the colonial authorities of this country, now sits gathering dust in the bowels of some British museum.

The mortal remains of an estimated three thousand Indigenous Australians remain stored in British museums.[140] All should be repatriated to their Country and their people.

Australia Day

The celebration of Australia Day on 26th January each year is a source of much bitter division, sometimes even violent division, between white and Indigenous Australians. Every year, graffiti is sprayed or daubed on public walls and monuments by Aboriginal activists, urging the nation to "Change The Date!" Every year Indigenous people conduct noisy protest marches calling on the government to "Change The Date!" Yet, prime ministers, have consistently refused to do so. They know that, no matter what date they might choose, it would be a divisive issue. For them, it is a poisoned chalice that threatens to damage their political capital. Many Aboriginal people claim that the celebration should be abolished completely, that it is the concept of celebrating white colonisation of this land which is the problem, not the date. They are right.

Not only is 26th January the anniversary of "Invasion Day", the date that Governor Arthur Phillip raised the British flag at Sydney Cove and established the Colony of New South Wales, it is also the anniversary of the massacre at Slaughterhouse Creek and the anniversary of the overthrow of Governor William Bligh in Australia's only political coup. It is a date that is not worthy of celebration for Indigenous *or* for non-Indigenous Australians. It is, in so many ways, not a propitious day.

This nation needs to ask, "What do we want our national day to look like? What do we want it to mean? What is it that we want to celebrate? Do we want to celebrate the beginning of a long and bloody war for survival? Do we want to celebrate conquest and subjugation, or would we rather celebrate national unity?

It is my opinion that Australia Day in its current form and on its current date should be abolished until such time as we have something worth celebrating – something that all Australians, black *and* white can celebrate together. Perhaps, if the government moves to make a national apology to Indigenous people as suggested earlier in this chapter, then *that* would be something worth celebrating. Perhaps we could all celebrate "Reconciliation Day".

Reconciliation Day

Perhaps, in fact, there is already a worthy date for Reconciliation Day. In 1993, faith communities across Australia commenced a "Week of Prayer for Reconciliation". In 1996, that Week of Prayer for Reconciliation was formally adopted as "National Reconciliation Week".[141] Most non-Indigenous Australians pay little heed to National Reconciliation Week which occurs annually from 27th May to 3rd June, two significant dates in Indigenous and non-Indigenous relations. The first of those dates, 27th May, is the anniversary of the 1967 referendum which recognised Indigenous people as Australian citizens and included them in the national census counts. The second, 3rd June, is the anniversary of the 1992 High Court judgment in the Mabo case, recognising that Indigenous peoples had lived in Australia for many thousands of years and enjoyed rights to their land according to their own laws and customs.

Effectively, Mabo overturned the myth that, at the time of colonisation, this nation was *terra nullius*.

A date in the middle of that week, perhaps 1st June annually, might be an appropriate date for Reconciliation Day. The choosing of such a date in itself would not be enough to ensure true and complete reconciliation, but perhaps together with the abolition of Australia Day, with a national apology and with some of the other measures mentioned above, it would bring us close to complete healing and reconciliation.

10
MAKARRATA

This land, home to Aboriginal peoples for more than sixty thousand years, is now a land shared by those Indigenous peoples and those who have come from many nations, making Australia one of the most multicultural nations in the world. That is now *fait accompli* – the clock cannot be turned back, and nobody suggests that all non-Indigenous Australians should pack up and leave. What we must do is quite simple – we must learn to live together.

Constitutional Recognition

It was not until 1965 that Aboriginal people were given a place at the ballot box in this country – the right to vote in every federal and state election across Australia. Later, a referendum on 27th May 1967 finally recognised them as Australian citizens and included them in the national census. It is to the shame of white Australia that it took more than 175 years to count Indigenous Australians as part of the Australian community in their own land.

On 26th May 2017, delegates to the First Nations National Constitutional Convention met for four days in the shadows of Uluru in Central Australia, seeking to determine how Aboriginals and Torres Strait Islanders could truly be part of the Australian community. At the conclusion of the Convention, a statement was released, in effect a petition, calling on Australians to make constitutional change, to establish a Voice to Parliament through which the concerns of Indigenous Australians could be heard. They entitled the petition *The Uluru Statement From The Heart*. Virtually all Australians have heard of this statement. Few have actually read it.

THE ULURU STATEMENT

FROM THE HEART

We, gathered at the 2017 National Constitutional Convention, coming from all points of the southern sky, make this statement from the heart:

Our Aboriginal and Torres Strait Islander tribes were the first Sovereign Nations of the Australian continent and its adjacent islands and possessed it under our own laws and customs. This our ancestors did, according to the reckoning of our culture, from the Creation, according to the common law from 'time immemorial', and according to science more than 60,000 years ago.

This Sovereignty is a spiritual notion: the ancestral tie between the land, or 'mother nature', and the Aboriginal and Torres Strait Islander peoples who were born therefrom, remain attached thereto, and must one day return thither to be united with our ancestors. This link is the basis of the ownership of the soil, or better, of Sovereignty. It has never been ceded or extinguished and co-exists with the Sovereignty of the Crown.

How could it be otherwise? That peoples possessed a land for sixty millennia and this sacred link disappears from world history in merely the last two hundred years?

With substantive constitutional change and structural reform, we believe this ancient Sovereignty can shine through as a fuller expression of Australia's nationhood.

Proportionally, we are the most incarcerated people on the planet. We are not an innately criminal people. Our children are aliened from their families at unprecedented rates. This cannot be because we have no love for them. And our youth languish in detention in obscene numbers. They should be our hope for the future.

> *These dimensions of our crisis tell plainly the structural nature of our problem. This is the torment of our powerlessness.*
>
> *We seek constitutional reforms to empower our people and take a rightful place in our own country. When we have power over our destiny our children will flourish. They will walk in two worlds and their culture will be a gift to their country.*
>
> *We call for the establishment of a First Nations Voice enshrined in the Constitution.*
>
> *Makarrata is the culmination of our agenda: the coming together after a struggle. It captures our aspirations for a fair and truthful relationship with the people of Australia and a better future for our children based on justice and self-determination.*
>
> *We seek a Makarrata Commission to supervise a process of agreement-making between governments and First Nations and truth-telling about our history.*
>
> *In 1967 we were counted, in 2017 we seek to be heard. We leave base camp and start our trek across this vast country. We invite you to walk with us in a movement of the Australian people for a better future.*[142]

On 23rd May 2022, the Australian people elected a new federal government – a Labor government led by Prime Minister Anthony Albanese. One of Albanese's core promises and one of his first statements on assuming office was that his government would "implement in full" the provisions of The Uluru Statement From The Heart, including the call for the establishment of a First Nations Voice enshrined in the Constitution.

The reason for seeking to have the Voice enshrined in the Australian Constitution was to ensure that it would endure beyond the term of any elected federal government. Too often in the past, Indigenous advisory and management bodies have been disbanded and abolished by new incoming governments. To have the Voice enshrined in the constitution, however, would require the successful carriage of a referendum for a referendum is the only way to change the Constitution. If carried, the Voice could then only be removed or disbanded by the carriage of yet another referendum.

Yet, getting a referendum approved in Australia is not an easy process. The Australian Constitution can be amended only with the approval of Australian electors, approved by a "double majority" – a national majority of all electors in the states and territories across the nation, and a majority of electors in a majority of states, that is, a majority in at least four of the six states. Since Federation in 1901, forty-five referendums to change the constitution have been put before the Australian people. When the Albanese government set the date for the referendum on the Voice, 14th October 2023, only eight of those forty-five referendums had been carried, and no referendum had ever been carried without the bipartisan support of the major political parties. [143]

The proposal put forward by the Albanese government asked the Australian people to amend the Constitution by inserting the following clauses:

1. There shall be a body, to be called the Aboriginal and Torres Strait Islander Voice.

2. The Aboriginal and Torres Strait Islander Voice may make representations to Parliament and to Executive Government on matters relating to Aboriginal and Torres Strait Islander Peoples.

3. The Parliament shall, subject to this Constitution, have power to make laws with respect to the composition,

functions, powers and procedures of the Aboriginal and Torres Strait Islander Voice.

Under the proposed constitutional change, the Voice would have had no executive or legislative powers, nor would it have had power of veto over any government legislation or initiative. Its role would have been solely to provide advice to the Parliament and Executive Government on policies and projects that would impact the lives of Aboriginal and Torres Strait Islander people. Such advice could have been accepted or rejected by the parliament. It was a simple proposal to better the lives of Aboriginal people and those of their children – it asked little of white Australians, yet it had so much to offer in terms or reconciliation. It was long overdue.

Almost immediately, the leader of the Australian National Party, David Littleproud (perhaps not an inappropriate name), announced that the National Party would oppose the proposed referendum. He was followed in like manner, soon after, by Peter Dutton, leader of the Australian Liberal Party. Because no referendum in Australian history has ever been passed without bipartisan political support, the referendum was effectively killed off at that point, along with any chance of true reconciliation.

Yes, in politics the role of an opposition party is to oppose – that is why they are called "the Opposition". Yet there are some things which should be above politics – issues of justice, fairness, human dignity, common decency and national unity. When the conservative side of politics in this country chose to campaign against the referendum which sought to give First Nations Peoples a Voice enshrined in our constitution, they were announcing their determination to hijack what should have been a community process and make it a political process for their own cynical political agenda. In doing so, they were choosing to entrench the status quo, which has kept this nation divided since white settlement in 1788, and to deny the aspirations of the vast majority of Indigenous people in this land.

On 14th October 2023, the Australian people overwhelmingly voted against the proposed change to the constitution, opting for no change and entrenching the black-white divide that this nation has lived with since 1788. The reasons were wide and varied. Some voted "No" because of an underlying racist attitude that still pervades this country. Others voted "No" out of fear – totally unfounded fear that, if the referendum were passed, white Australians would lose their right to free speech, or perhaps they might even lose their homes. There were even rumours circulating within the community and stoked by those campaigning for a "No" vote, that white Australians would be banned or would have to pay to enter public places, such as Bondi Beach. Some voted out of selfishness. "Why should they have something I don't have?" was a commonly heard objection to the proposed constitutional change. A large part of the blame for the failure of the referendum, however, must be sheeted home to the conservative side of politics in this country. Not only did they officially campaign against the referendum, they promoted misinformation and fear amongst the Australian populace. Shame on them!

The Indigenous people of this land have been slapped in the face. They reached out their hand in reconciliation to white Australia, and the nation turned its back on them. Yet, they will get through this. They are gentle and resilient people who have had almost two hundred and fifty years to become accustomed to rejection. It has happened before, it likely will happen again. They are used to it.

The proposed Indigenous Voice to parliament should not have been about political opportunism. It was a unique opportunity for this country to come together, united in purpose, to provide a better future for all Australians. Politicians who campaigned against a "Yes" vote were seeking to deny this nation any chance of true national reconciliation and score points against their political opponents.

A successful "Yes" vote would not have undone all the wrongs which have been perpetrated against Indigenous Australians since 26th January 1788 but it may have determined the kind of country we would all live in going forward. It should have been incumbent on those who opposed it to not only say "No!" but to propose their own way forward. Yet, they did not. They simply said "No!" and campaigned against the proposed Voice. In doing so, they rejected the hand of reconciliation that had been extended by the first peoples of this land.

Despite the failure of the referendum on the Voice, the winds of change do occasionally blow across this nation like a gentle zephyr that too often falls away in fragility – stifled by people who say "No". Yet, green shoots of hope appear now and then, here and there, the promise that people, white Australians, are very gradually becoming more open to learning about the dark side of our history – about how to manage it and how to live with it. In the year 2000, a quarter of a million people, black and white, walked across Sydney Harbour Bridge in unison and in support of national reconciliation.[145] Unfortunately, more than twenty years later, that initiative has been all but forgotten, and the opportunity it presented has been lost. In 2023, we have seen another opportunity lost – reconciliation between our black and white citizens has been set back for at least a generation, and it hurts.

Reconciliation, the process of peoples coming together to acknowledge injustices and to embrace one another as peoples with a shared future, can be long and painful. It may take years, decades and sometimes centuries – progress can be agonisingly slow. But those who hope in a united future must remain resilient and seize the next opportunity when it comes along so that our children and our children's children, need not live in a nation divided. Right now, however, at the time of writing, those who believe in the reconciliation of our black and white citizens are hurting – they are greatly saddened by the failure of the Voice Referendum.

Yet another enormous opportunity has been lost – an opportunity to make the lives of all Australians, black and white, more equal in terms of living standards and many socio-economic indicators in a variety of areas – health, addictions, education, employment opportunities, housing, incarceration rates, deaths in custody rates and suicide rates. The baton for such change has now been passed to the next generation. May the young people of the next generation prove more worthy than the people of the present generation.

Poor Fellow My Country.[146]

CITATIONS

A number of documents cited in this work were originally handwritten in the eighteenth and nineteenth centuries. Fortunately for readers and researchers, the documents have been digitised and/or scanned for online access. In some cases, they have been scanned by numerous institutions, each producing files in different formats.

1   The writings of Judge Advocate, David Collins, *An Account of the English Colony in New South Wales* is a most valuable work, essential for any person researching this period of Australian history. The work, which is in two volumes, is accessible from the following sources:

- The University of Sydney has two digitised text-based versions which can be viewed online: Vol 1 published 1798 and Vol 2 published 1804.

- The same two volumes are also available through Project Gutenberg, an initiative focused on digitising out of print works. Their versions have multiple formats and include both text and images.

- The National Library of Australia (Canberra) has a digitised version which can be accessed through the NLA online catalogue with an NLA membership card.

- The State Library of New South Wales has a digitised album which includes high quality scans of the original (handwritten) work.

- Google Books has digitised print versions of both Volumes

Of course, finding the same piece of quoted text in these different digitised versions of the same work will give different page numbers as references, depending upon the institution from which the document is sourced. It, therefore, seems necessary to inform the reader about which document source has been chosen and cited in this work.

In this book, references to David Collins' *An Account of the English Colony in New South Wales* has been sourced from the Google Books digitised versions (see URLs below) and page number references refer to the Google Books versions.

Vol 1   Collins An Account of the English Colony in New South Wales, Cadell and Davies, London 1798
https://books.google.com.au/books?id=eRZcAAAAcAAJ&printsec=frontcover&source=gbs_ge_summary_r&cad=0#v=onepage&q&f=false

Vol 2   Collins An Account of the English Colony in New South Wales, Cadell and Davies, London 1804
https://books.google.com.au/books?id=ol5dAAAAcAAJ&pg=PA288&redir_esc=y#v=onepage&q&f=false

2.   Watkin Tench's book, *A Narrative Of The Expedition To Botany Bay*, Debrett, London, 1789 (another invaluable resource) has been accessed in digital format through the State Library of NSW:

https://www.sl.nsw.gov.au/collection-items/narrative-expedition-botany-bay-account-new-south-wales-its-productions-inhabitants

References

1. *Sydney Gazette &New South Wales Advertiser*, 21 April 1805, p.2

2. VOC – Verenigde Oostindische Compagnie. The Dutch East India Company

3. Hints offered for the consideration of Captain Cook are preserved in the National Library of Australia's Manuscript Collection, along with Cook's handwritten journal. These were "hints" given to Cook by the President of the Royal Society, James Douglas, 14th Earl of Morton

4. Ingrey, Shane, *Voices Heard But Not Understood* https://www.gujaga.org.au/stories/voices-heard-but-not-understood
(accessed October 2022)

5. *Cook's Journals – Daily Entries*, 29 April 1770 http://southseas.nla.gov.au/journals/cook/17700429.html
(accessed October 2022)

6. *Cook's Journals – Daily Entries*, 30 April 1770 http://southseas.nla.gov.au/journals/cook/17700430.html (accessed October 2022)

7. *Cook's Journals – Daily Entries*, 6 May 1770 http://southseas.nla.gov.au/journals/cook/17700506.html (accessed October 2022)

8. Ibid.

9. Ibid.

10. *Cook's Journals – Daily Entries*, 21 August 1770 http://southseas.nla.gov.au/journals/cook/17700821.html (accessed October 2022)

11. *Cook's Journals – Daily Entries*, 22 August 1770 http://southseas.nla.gov.au/journals/cook/17700822.html (accessed October 2022)

12. Ibid.

13. Edwards, P (ed), *JAMES COOK – The Journals* Prepared from the original manuscripts by J. C. Beaglehole for the Hakluyt Society, 1955-67. Selected and edited by Philip Edwards. Penguin Classics, London 1999. p174

14. Lord Sydney, Instructions for Governor Arthur Phillip, 25 April 1787, p.16 NOTE: original document handwritten on 6 [size] pages. Digitised version is available on the website of the Queensland University of Technology (QUT) https://digitalcollections.qut.edu.au/4738/ (accessed November 2022)

15. Pascoe, Bruce, *Dark Emu*, Magabala Books Aboriginal Corporation, Broome, WA, 2014 (second edition 2018)

16. Ibid. p.7

17. Ibid. p.25

18. See:
Sutton, Peter and Walshe, Keryn, *Farmers or Hunter-Gathers? The Dark Emu Debate*, Melbourne University Press, 2022
    and
Rintoul, Stuart. *Debunking Dark Emu: did the publishing phenomenon get it wrong?*, Sydney Morning Herald, 12 June 2021. https://www.smh.com.au/national/debunking-dark-emu-did-the- publishing-phenomenon-get-it-wrong-20210507-p57pyl.html (accessed February 2023)

19. Pascoe, op. cit. p.19

20. Pascoe, op. cit. p.8

21. Pascoe, op. cit. p.9

22. Tench, W, *A Narrative of the Expedition to Botany Bay*, Debrett, London 1789, p.53

23. Collins, David. *An Account of the English Colony in New South Wales*. Libraries Board of South Australia, Adelaide, 1971, Cadell & Davies, London, 1798, vol. 1, p.58

24. Ibid. Appendix No 5. p.559

25. Tench, W, op. cit., p.57-58

26. Bradley, William. *A Voyage to New South Wales* December 1786 – May 1792. Compiled by William Bradley, pp.181-183

27. Tench, W, *A Complete Account of the Settlement at Port Jackson in New South Wales, including an Accurate Description of the Colony, of the Natives, and of its Natural Productions*, Nicol & Sewell, London, 1793, p,.35

28. Flynn, Michael, *Second Fleet*, Dictionary of Sydney, 2016, http://dictionaryofsydney.org/entry/second_fleet. (accessed Sep 2021)

29. W. Hill to Jonathan Watham Esq. of Bond Court, Walbrook, London, dated Sydney Cove, Port Jackson, 26th. July 1790. Now held in the Mitchell Library, State Library of New South Wales.

30. Tench, W. op.cit., p,.36

31. Karskens, Grace, *The Colony: A History of Early Sydney*, Allen & Unwin, Sydney, 2009, p.454

32. Collins, David. op,cit., p.148

33. Tench, W, *A Complete Account of the Settlement at Port Jackson*, published as *Sydney's First Four Years* edited by L. F. Fitzhardinge, Library of Australian History, Sydney, 1979, pp. 95-102

34. Ibid

35. The Morning Post (London), 10 June 1793

36. Lloyds Evening Post (London) 29 May 1793

37. The Observer (London) 28 September 1793

38. The Oracle and Public Advertiser (London) 16 April 1794

39. Grose to Dundas, 29 April 1794, Historical Records of Australia (HRA), Series 1, vol.1 (1788-1796), p.469

40. Ibid. p.470

41. Chisolm, A, Wilson, John (?-1800) in *Australian Dictionary of Biography*, https://adb.anu.edu.au/biography/wilson-john-2803 (accessed December 2022)

42. Atkins, Richard, Journal, 15 April 1794. Quoted in *Incidents between Aboriginal people in NSW and the British colonisers 1792-1809*. www.nationalunitygovernment.org › pdf › 2014 (accessed October 2022)

43. Ibid.

44. Collins, David, op.cit., p.390 (Google books digitised version)

45. Ibid. p.394

46. *Paterson to Henry Dundas*, HRA Series 1, vol.1 (1797-1796) p.499

47. Collins David, op.cit. p.416

48. *Paterson to Henry Dundas*, op. cit., HRA Series 1, vol.1 (1797-1796) p.499

49. *Collins to Edward Laing*,11 June 179, Kings Papers (b) Mitchell Library of New South Wales Sydney .131134, as quoted by John Currey in David Collins: *A Colonial Life*, Melbourne, Miegunyah Press, 2000, p.126

50. *Paterson to Henry Dundas*, op. cit. HRA Series 1, vol 1 (1797-1796) p.499

51. Collins, David, op.cit. p.228

52. Macintyre, Stuart, *A Concise History of Australia*, Cambridge University Press, Cambridge 199, p.8

53. *Hunter to Duke of Portland* 6 July 1797. *Historical Records of Australia* (HRA), Series 1, vol 2 p.82

54. Collins, David, 1804, p.442

55. Collins, David, 1798, p.394

56. Collins, David, 1804, p.275

57. *Hunter to Duke of Portland*, 1 November 1798, HRA Series1, vol.2 (1797-1800) pp.236-237

58. "The Savoy" was a military prison situated near the site where Waterloo Bridge now spans the River Thames.

59. HRNSW Vol. 3 (1796-1799) p.65

60. Hunter to Duke of Portland, 2 February 1800, HRA Series 1, vol 2, pp.411-412

61. Ibid. p.402

62. Ibid.

63. Ibid.

64. Ibid. pp.403-422

65. HRA Series 1, vol. 2 (1797-1800) p.14

66. *Macarthur to Portland*, HRA Series 1, vol.2 (1797-1800, p.91

67. HRA Series 1, vol. 2 (1797-1800), p. x (Introduction)

68. *Hunter to King* HRNSW Vol. 4 (1800, 1801, 1802) p.171

69. HRA Series 1, vol. 2 (1797-1800) p.402

70. HRA Series 1, vol. 1, p.14

71. Ibid. pp.124-128

72. HRA Series 1, vol. 3 (1801-1802) p.322

73. HRA Series 1, vol. 5 (July 1804 – August 1806), p.552

74. See pp.82-4 of this work

75. Estensen, Miriam, *The Life of George Bass*, Allen & Unwin, Melbourne 2005, p.72

76. HRA Series 1, vol. 3, p.257

77. King, Philip Gidley. Government & General Order, 1 May 1801. HRNSW vol 4, p.362

78. Caley to Banks, 25 August 1801, HRNSW Vol. 4, pp.:513–4

79. HRA Series 1, vol. 3 (1801-1802), p.466

80. HRNSW vol. 4 (1800, 1801, 1802) p.629

81. King to Portland, 1 March 1802 HRA Series 1, vol. 3 (1801 - 1802), p.467

82. King to Lord Hobart, HRNSW vol. 4 (1800, 1801, 1802) pp.867-868

83. Ibid.

84. *Australian Institution of Aboriginal and Torres Strait Islander (1 January 2001). Aboriginal Sydney : a guide to important places of the past and present. Aboriginal Studies Press. p. 141.*

85. *King to Banks, HRNSW vol 4, p.784*

86. *David Collins to Under Secretary Sullivan 27 December 1802, HRNSW vol 4 (1800, 1801, 1802) p.629 p.926*

87. Kohen J.L, *Pemulwuy*, in Australian Dictionary of Biography, https://adb.anu.edu.au/biography/pemulwuy-13147 (accessed November 2022).

88. Ibid.

89. *Sydney Gazette & New South Wales Advertiser*, 17 June 1804, p.2

90. Ibid.

91. King to Lord Hobart, 20th December 1804, HRNSW Vol. 5 (1803-1805) p.513

92. *Sydney Gazette & New South Wales Advertiser*, 21 April 1805, p.2

93. Ibid.

94. *Sydney Gazette & New South Wales Advertiser*, 16 June 1805, p.2

95. See page 75

96. *Sydney Gazette & New South Wales Advertiser*, 23 June 1805, p.2

97. *Sydney Gazette & New South Wales Advertiser*, 12 January 1806, p.1

98. King to Earl Camden, 15 March 1806, HRNSW vol. 6 (1806, 1807, 1808), p.42

99. Governor King, as quoted and related by Shaw, A.G.L. in King, Philip Gidley (1758-1808) in Australian Dictionary of Biography, https://adb.anu.edu.au/biography/king-philip-gidley-2309 (accessed December 2022)

100. Ibid.

101.HRNSW vol. 4 (1800, 1801, 1802) pp.362

102.*Sydney Gazette & New South Wales Advertiser*, 12 May 1805, p.2

103.Ibid.

104.HRA, Series 1, vol. 7 (January 1809 – June 1813), p.192

105.Government & General Order, *Sydney Gazette & New South Wales Advertiser*, 7 January 1810, p.1

106.Karskens, Grace. Appin Massacre. https://dictionaryofsydney.org/entry/appin_massacre . (Accessed December 2022)

107.Hale, P. & Koeneman, T. *Rethinking Governor Macquarie's Aboriginal Policy*, Heritage Council of New South Wales, https://web.archive.org/web/20170918083943/http://www.environment.nsw.gov.au/resources/heritagebranch/heritage/govmacquarieaboriginalpolicy.pdf

108.HRA Series 1, vol. 8 p.313

109.Governor Macquarie to Earl Bathurst. (note 70) HRA Series 1, vol.8, p.368

110.Ibid. p.369

111.Ibid. p373

112.Government & General Order, Government House Sydney, 10 December 1814. Establishment of the Native Institution.

113.*Sydney Gazette & New South Wales Advertiser*, 17 December 1814, p.2

114.Ibid.

115.Hale, P. & Koeneman, T, op. cit., p.4

116.*Sydney Gazette & New South Wales Advertiser*, 31 December 1814, p.2

117.*Sydney Gazette & New South Wales Advertiser*, 4 January 1817, pp.2-3

118.Macquarie, Lachlan. *Diary, 10 April 1816 – 1 July 1818.* Original held in the Mitchell Library, Sydney: ML Ref: A773 pp.1-8. [Microfilm Reel CY301 Frames #237-245].

119.Karskens, G, *The Colony* op. cit. p.508

120. Hale, P & Koeneman, T, op-cit. pp.5-6

121. Macquarie, Lachlan, op. cit.

122. Proclamation by Macquarie, *Sydney Gazette & New South Wales Advertiser*, 11 May 1816, p.1

123. Macquarie to Lord Bathurst, 8 June 1816, HRA Series 1, vol.9, pp.139140

124. Report of the Commissioner of Inquiry into the state of the colony of New South Wales. State Library of NSW. https://digital.sl.nsw.gov.au/delivery/DeliveryManagerServlet?embedded=true&toolbar=false&dps_pid=IE3735574 (accessed January 2023)

125. Ibid.

126. Aboriginal Studies Press, 2016

127. The full interview can be listened to online at https://www.abc.net.au/radionational/programs/breakfast/most-Indigenous-people-will-call-for-statues-to-be-removed/8851536

128. https://c21ch.newcastle.edu.au/colonialmassacres/

129. https://c21ch.newcastle.edu.au/colonialmassacres/map.php

130. *Sydney Gazette & New South Wales Advertiser*, 12 May 1805, p. 2

131. Ryan, Lyndall," *Tasmanian Aborigines*, Allen & Unwin, Sydney, 2012, pp. 14 & 43

132. *Colonial Times*, Hobart, 1 December 1826, p.2

133. Ryan, Lyndall. op. cit., pp.87-91 and 123-124

134. Ibid. pp.93-100

135. Aborigines of Van Diemen's Land: Copy of Dispatch from Lt.Gov. Arthur to Mr. Sec. Huskisson, 17th April 1828. *Parliamentary Papers, House of Commons and Command, Volume 19. 1831. p. 5.*

136. *Colonial Times*, Hobart, 1 December 1826, p.2

137. Australian Bureau of Statistics

138. *Evening News*, Sydney, 7 October 1899, p.4

139. *Bradley, Michael. Coniston. Perth, 2019, UWA Publishing*

140. *Heathcote, Angela. "On this day: Pemulwuy is killed." Australian Geographic, 1 June 2017*

141. What you need to know about reconciliation https://www.creativespirits.info/aboriginalculture/peopl e/what-you-need-to-know-about-reconciliation#what-is-the-national-reconciliation-week-about (Accessed December 2022)

142. https://ulurustatement.org/

143. Australian Electoral Commission https://www.aec.gov.au/Elections/referendums/Refere ndum_Dates_and_Results.htm (Accessed December 2022)

144. The Australia Institute, "Polling – Voice to Parliament in the Constitution", July 2022. https://australiainstitute.org.au/report/polling-voice-to-parliament-in-the-constitution/ (Accessed December 2022)

145. "What you need to know about reconciliation" op. cit.

146. Herbert, Xavier, *Poor Fellow My Country*, Collins, Australia 1975

INDEX